A Nation's Holocaust and Betrayal
Ireland 1172–1992

A Nation's Holocaust and Betrayal
Ireland 1172–1992

Michael L Redmond

The Pentland Press Limited
Edinburgh • Cambridge • Durham

First published in 1994 by
The Pentland Press Ltd.
1 Hutton Close
South Church
Bishop Auckland
Durham

ISBN 1 85821 219 7

Typeset by CBS, Felixstowe, Suffolk
Printed and bound by Antony Rowe Ltd., Chippenham

This book is dedicated to the memory
of the millions of Irish men and women
who perished at home and abroad
as a result of the holocaust forced on them.

Remember them always.

ACKNOWLEDGEMENTS

In writing this book I have received most generous help from my family. I owe special praise to my sisters – Sr. Margaret, Sr. Katherine and Mrs. Mary Lundy and to my brother Thomas who gave their valuable time in assisting me, to my daughters Rosemarie, for all the patience she endured typing and retyping of the manuscript, to Deborah for her expertise in arranging the sections of the book and all the time she spent in typing my letters to publishers and others. I owe my grateful thanks to the Librarian and staff of the Wexford Library for their courtesy and valuable help.

CONTENTS

CHAPTER 1

A HISTORY OF IRELAND FROM 1172 TO THE TUDOR PERIOD 1558

I quote abstracts from Eleanor Hall's, *History of Ireland* volume i.
In my opinion there is little doubt that from AD 432 to 1772 Medieval Ireland was ruled by Irish clans, kings, earls and chieftains with the help of some Europeans. It may surprise many that Patrick (our Saint) was a Roman soldier and he was not the first to bring Christianity to Ireland for it was here before he arrived. It is more likely that he was sent here to prepare the way for a Roman conquest.

It would, therefore, be fair to say that, throughout this period whatever occurred by the ongoing inter wars among the clans and chieftains, the English Establishment had no great power or influence in Ireland. On the other hand, the Irish chieftains and clans took an active part in the local wars in England, Scotland and Wales.

In the year 1172 Pope Adrian I gave approval to King Henry II's claim to rule Ireland. This claim being confirmed by Pope Alexander III – The Bull of Adrian 1172. The English Conquest of Ireland began and steadily it proceeded until Queen Elizabeth came to the English throne on the death of Queen Mary in the year 1558. From this period onwards the full weight of the English Establishment came to bear on Ireland and the first crimes committed by England against the Irish people can justifiably be said to take effect from this period.

CHAPTER 2

THE HISTORY OF IRELAND
FROM 1558 – 1912 (STUART PERIOD)

I quote the following abstracts from Eleanor Hall's *A History of Ireland* Volume ii.

On 24th October 1615, the Brehan Law in Ireland was abolished by the English Parliament and no other parliament sat in Ireland until Wentworth's Parliament of 1634.

In 1602 King James I's reign in Ireland was spent arranging the extra Plantations of Wexford, Wicklow, Monaghan, Fermanagh and Leitrim, also west of the Shannon. The Wexford Commission reported in 1613 that Kavanagh's land of 66,800 acres was claimed by the King on the surrender of Art McMurrough Kavanagh to Richard II. With the clans' systems gone and the Plantation of Ireland in progress (especially in Ulster) thousands of people, many who lost their land, were now roaming the country in order to exist and were ready to commit reprisals for the wrongs done to them. The English Establishment now feared that a rebellion was about to break out.

In 1605 Sir Arthur Chickenden is quoted as saying this recipe for the ills of Ireland, 'Famine to consume them... English manners to reform them... they starve miserable and eat dogs, mares where they can get them... when they are down it must be good laws, I have often written that it is famine that must consume them... our swords and other endeavours work not that speedy effect which is expected.'

In 1641 Sir Robert Talbot's petition to the King, says all Irish lands of the Pale, Catholic and Protestant, are loyal to England and to the Crown and against the rebellion in the confederate wars.

The Ormonde Peace resulted in the Pope of Rome appointing Rinuccini as Nuncio to Ireland. This period was dominated by wars and dictated by Rome who made the arrival of Cromwell's success a lot easier and with it the end of the feudal gentry and their wars in Ireland. On July 26th 1649 Oliver Cromwell and his army landed in Dublin and the slaughter of the people began. Wexford and Drogheda are the two main towns which met the worst of the killings and plunder. On the other hand he got rid of the Royalists and drove them west of the Shannon. People like Ormonde, Owen Roe O'Neill and many others including, the Catholic bishops, were all Royalists. Out of a population of one and a quarter million, 800,000 were Irish and 400,000 were English and Scots by 1672.

King James II landed at Kinsale, County Cork, on 12th March 1689 with up to 3,000 warships, with many support ships, around 2,000 guns, some 14,000 troops and half a million crowns in money.

The coming wars were between Catholic France and Protestant Holland. It was also the reason why William came to Ireland in 1690 to fight for the Crown of England. William's army was made up of Dutch, Swedes, Germans, Danes, English and Scottish armies while James II's army was mostly French and Irish.

On May 7th 1689 the Irish Parliament met in Dublin with James II present. Many Acts were passed, the most important declared, anew, the independence of the Irish Parliament – the preamble is as follows:

Where His Majesty's Realm of Ireland is and hath always been a distinct Kingdom from that of His Majesty's Realm of England, it is hereby declared that no Act of Parliament passed, or to be passed, in the Parliament of England, though Ireland should be therein mentioned, can be or shall be in any binde in Ireland.

The above declaration and the meaning of the said Act supplied the text for Swift and future leaders to claim the legal rights of the Irish Nation and the freedom of the Irish people.

James II's Irish campaign of 1690 was a disaster to the French and Irish, Colonel Kelly's account was that James' way of getting back England was to lose Ireland. By his actions on and off the battlefield this account to me is the case. He had no intention of helping Catholic Ireland but used her to get back the Throne of England.

The failure of James' army and his final defeat at Limerick in 1691 put paid to any peace in Ireland. With the departure of all the fine leaders and their families and soldiers to France, Ireland was now left in a very weak condition. It gave the final signal to England to take over Ireland completely and administer it by direct rule. James II had played a major part. This period 1689 – 1691 will be seen to be the most important and critical time for Ireland and the last chance was lost for the Irish to own and control their own country and to rid Ireland of all foreign armies for the next two hundred and thirty years.

Arthur Young commenting in 1776 as an agricultural expert wrote, that it required the American War of Independence to awaken England to the results of her narrow trading policy towards her colonies under which America, the Indies and Ireland were equally suffering. The poor Irish population had only potatoes and sour milk to live on and a series of famines showed the level at which the people were existing. This resulted in the starvation of almost half a million people in 1741.

Jonathan Swift, Dean of St. Patrick, in the year 1724, seeing the depressed state of the country and the wretched conditions of the poor wrote 'Were not the people of Ireland born as free of those of England? How have they forfeited their freedom? – Am I a freeman of England and do I become a slave in six hours in crossing the channel? I have looked all over English and Irish statutes without finding any law that makes Ireland depend upon England any more than England does upon Ireland, for in reason on all governments without the consent of the governed is the very definition of slavery, but in fact eleven men well armed will certainly subdue one single man in his shirt.'

Swift exposed the illegal English claim in Ireland in law. He was born in Dublin in 1667, died in 1745, and had one of the most brilliant minds of his time.

THE VOLUNTEERS RISING

With the volunteers arming for a rebellion, the English became very alarmed. Eden gave an account of the present affairs in Ireland to the House of Commons and urged the House to agree to all the measures proposed by the volunteers. With Gratten as their spokesman, it proves yet again only when England feels insecure will Ireland benefit.

On 21st June 1782 the Act of Repeal was passed in the House of

Commons and a Bill and an Act of Renunciation passed expressly resigned all rights of the English over the Irish Parliament. There was this great question settled – as was then supposed.

'Gratten Parliament' as it became known only lasted for a very short time. The English Government at a stroke, as it had done before and since, dismissed the powers of the Irish Parliament and together with her allies namely the Protestant Irish, the Irish gentry, Catholic bishops and landlords declared war on the Irish Republican Movement. The English were trying to invoke this war for a long time in order to cement 'the Union by force permanently'. John Fitzgibbon (later Earl of Clare) was appointed agent by Pitt to set the Union in place with the buying and selling of the Irish Members of Parliament votes for large sums of money. As the reward for this success, he was appointed Attorney-General for Ireland by Pitt in 1783.

Gratten, being a Royalist, agreed by an Indemnity Bill (an Insurrection Act) to absolve all magistrates from the consequences of their acts if suppressing any order of the said acts. This act became law in Ireland in 1796.

With at least 50,000 troops in the country, the Habeas Corpus Act suspended all rights of assembly and denied discussion. Trials by court martial were the order of the day, the crimes and torture against the Irish people were once again put into action.

It is understood that it cost the English the sum of £600,000 in bribes to buy the Irish Protestant Parliament members votes. In order to give some respectability to their actions, they said all the Irish people were in favour of 'The Union', but they neglected to mention that the people had no vote and as a result the Act of Union of 1800, as passed, was illegal.

Wolfe Tone summed up the position as follows: 'The influence of England was the Radical Voice of our government,' and that, 'Ireland would never be quite free, prosperous or happy until she was independent'. Sir Henry Cavendish is quoted as saying 'That if Wolfe Tone were serious he ought to be hanged'.

It is said by many authors that Daniel O'Connell dedicated his life's work for the good of Ireland and its poor. He was a large landlord and member of the House of Parliament in England. He represented the Catholic Church and all the upper classes within the Pale and his luxury life style was borne on the backs of the poor whose interests he had not.

Some would say he and the Catholic bishops were traitors to their people and country. It would seem to the writer they were agents for the English and used their superior education and abilities to give the impression that they were great and noble Irishmen.

It has just been announced by the Central Bank of Ireland that Daniel O'Connell is to be honoured on the new twenty punt note. This undertaking highlights the position that nothing has changed much over the past one hundred and fifty years.

Prior to the Act of Union of 1800 Ireland had made some good progress in expanding trade and industry, it is very difficult to understand many authors' assessments that the problem of the land wars, rent, price of land and so on was the fault of 'Old Customs' among the Irish going back to the feudal times.

Is it not a fact that post 1800 Britain had complete control over Ireland and ruled her directly from London and had full control and power in making and changing laws for Ireland at a stroke of a pen when she so wished? The authors, therefore, would seem to be saying that Britain had no say in such matters. By ignoring the obvious, many authors sat on the fence and in doing so made sure that Britain be exonerated throughout the world for the crimes and policy she forced on the Irish people.

The legacy of 1798 is a story of incredible bravery and brutality and yet despite its failures the united Irishmen's movement influenced the thinking of later generations to continue the struggle for an Irish Republic as outlined by Wolfe Tone.

THE YOUNG IRELAND AND THE FENIANS

The leaders of the movement, and in particular John Mitchel, had great hopes that at last the country had a movement in size and a system which had the support of the majority and would be a major threat to the British. Yet again, as we see many times before, the Catholic bishops, informers and the 'Pale People', being agents for the British, betrayed the cause in the years 1842 – 1850.

It should also be noted that, at this time millions of Irish poor were starving to death by the great Holocaust which Britain had forced on the country. Great credit and courage by the movement under those conditions was not lost on future generations as we will see at later stages in this book.

I have pointed out in previous sections of the book that both Daniel O'Connell and the bishops were opposed to anything that could be called Nationalism or freedom for the masses. All they were interested in were the big grants for Maynooth Seminary of up to £35,000 a year becoming a permanent sum and other big grants to other colleges and universities.

O'Connell's credibility was put to the test by the biggest meeting to be held in Ireland at Clontarf. He called off the meeting when Peel banned it, saying he did so to avoid bloodshed. After spending six months in jail on a twelve month sentence for conspiracy in February 1844, he died on the way to Rome on 15th May 1847 at Genoa.

John Mitchel and other leaders were sentenced to fourteen years in Australia for treason on 1st April 1848.

THE LAND BILL

On 9th August 1870 the Land Bill was brought before the House of Commons by Gladstone and passed into law. It gave the Irish tenants compensation for improvements they carried out on landlords' estates. When evicted they were to be recompensed by the landlord, but the rent-rackets got worse in order that the landlords were not to be out of pocket; and, remember, those gentlemen were a law unto themselves.

On 22nd April 1875 Charles Stewart Parnell took his seat as a member for County Meath in the House of Commons. He took over control from Isaac Butt as leader of the Land League and for the first time Ireland had a leader who worried the British as to how much longer they could keep control of Ireland. He and the other leaders achieved this despite the freedom of the Catholic bishops to denounce them publicly from their safe haven of the pulpit. Parnell died in Brighton, England, on 6th October 1891, but beforehand he had passed on the torch to the next generation.

In 1857 John Redmond was born, his father being a landlord in County Wexford. He became leader of the Land League on the death of Parnell and continued to struggle for Home Rule for Ireland, but being part of the British Empire, he believed that Home Rule was just the start for Ireland to be free to manage her own affairs. As we have seen before, and will see again and again in the near future, Britain's 'Own Agenda' was not for the benefit of Ireland. Redmond's other problem was that he had agreed with the British to conscription of Irishmen into the Boer and First World Wars. This was a major mistake as the mood in Ireland had become more hostile to the British Establishment and the people were ready to fight them in Ireland for their independence. The Catholic bishops were also a problem for him. Unlike Parnell who denounced the bishops for their interference, Redmond was a loyalist and monarchist as was the Catholic Church.

With the advance on Sinn Fein, John Redmond and his Irish Party had lost their way and were out of step with the new Republican policy.

Having been deceived by the British, his loyalty to both camps was his downfall. He died on 6th March 1918.

HOME RULE BILL

Most authors state that there were three main causes why the Home Rule Bill was delayed, namely, Ulster, Sinn Féin and the First World War. I would say that Britain had never any intentions of granting Home Rule for the whole country of Ireland and the reasons put forward do not stand up to scrutiny. In September 1911 the Establishment in the north began to arm. The British turned a blind eye to the import of thirty thousand rifles and twenty thousand revolvers from Birmingham and on 24th April 1914 fifty thousand rifles and one million cartridges were landed at Larne and Bangor again with the blessing of the British. But the landing of arms at Howth in Dublin for the Irish Volunteers on 26th July 1914 led to military action and bloodshed and one can also recall some years before when Randolph Churchill declared to provide Ulster with a watchword with which to challenge Home Rule – 'Ulster will fight and Ulster will be right'.

Both Churchill and the Tory party pledged their support to Ulster in her resistance and when General Gough and fifty-seven of his officers at the Curragh Camp, County Kildare, refused to go north to carry out orders of the British government and was dismissed, no further action was taken to bring the northern leaders into line and uphold the law. This was further proof of Britain's intentions for both parts of Ireland and we will see later again how the British connivance with the northern leaders brought about the partition of Ireland.

The plans for the Easter Week Rising of 1916 by Pearse and other leaders was based on sound policy and noble principles. With Britain at war with Germany and the promise of Home Rule deferred and with Redmond's loyalty to the Crown, the leaders knew that a sacrifice of blood by them would light a flame for others to follow and win Irish freedom. Sinn Fein was now the force to do just that, in spite of their real enemy The Irish Catholic bishops.

The declaration of the Irish Republic in January 1919 was a direct result of the successful Rising of Easter 1916, which saw the leaders, sixteen in all, executed.

CHAPTER 3

COUNTY WEXFORD AND SURROUNDING AREAS 1750–1798

The following is based on Nicholas Furlong's book on the 1798 Rebellion, *Life in County Wexford and Adjoining Areas.*

With the Cromwellian victories in Ireland in the 1650s the Plantation of Ireland had begun and County Wexford, in particular the north and west of the county, was the area most affected by the English Royalists where the land was the best in the country. The Irish were now tenants to the landlords on their own land. The rents and tithes to the Church of England, being the Established Church, were far beyond the reach of most people. The misery and hardship that developed as a result caused conflicts on an ongoing basis and many people were tortured and killed, others put in jail.

The Revolution which took place on 14th July 1789 in France was the signal for the Irish people to organize themselves to rise up against the oppressor. The Catholic Church hierarchy was very concerned over what was happening in France, where king's, lords' and bishops' rule was overthrown. They lost no time in denouncing the United Irishmen's activities in recruiting members for the coming uprising. To quote Bishop James Caulfied of Ferns' statement on the matter, 'Such activities are contrary to the doctrine of Jesus Christ and his apostles and to all social and good order loyalty to our gracious good King George the Third'. It is little wonder that the English were in no hurry to destroy and eliminate the leaders of the United Irishmen as was the case in all previous uprisings, when they knew at all times that the Catholic bishops were their allies and agents and ready at all times to do their bidding without regard to what may happen to the people in order that they could hold on to power over the masses with the blessing of Rome and the English Establishment.

Bishop James Caulfield, in order to maintain his high standard of life style and power, denounced his own clergy. For example, he blamed Fr. John Murphy, leader of the 1798 rebellion, for the burning down of around thirty chapels in the county. At no time on the arrest of all the leaders, which included the clergy of County Wexford, did the bishop intervene in order to save them knowing, as he did, all of them would be executed. On the contrary, he sealed their fate by denouncing their actions as immoral and, as such, the work of the devil.

The 1798 Rising which took place only in the north of Ireland, Co. Cork, Co. Meath and Wexford was over and, to add to all previous failures, the people had now to soldier on in misery and hardship. Many had to flee the country to get away from the brutal oppression which now descended on the country by the English Establishment and there were no bounds to the torture they inflicted on the wretched Irish people. But, they failed as always to kill the spirit of the Irish who may have to wait until another time for the next rising. And a rising *there will be* until the English occupation of Ireland is overthrown.

CHAPTER 4

IRELAND BEFORE AND DURING
THE GREAT HOLOCAUST 1798 – 1850

The following is based on Gearoid O'Tuathaig's book, *Ireland Before and During the Famine.*

CENTRAL AND LOCAL GOVERNMENT

Dublin Castle was the centre of administration for the British machine, the royal representative being the Lord-Lieutenant who lived for part of each year in the Vice-Regal Lodge in the Pheonix Park. Law and order was their man pre-occupation throughout this period. The judges and grand juries were given greater powers and a lot of the corrupt corporations around the country were abolished.

LAW AND ORDER

All Court appointments from top to bottom were selected by the government and most were Protestants. Some reform was introduced during the period 1835 – 1840. In 1828 there was up to 35,000 regular soldiers. In addition there were 36,000 yeomanry, poorly disciplined, as was seen in the bloodshed they caused in 1798.

In 1830s some one-third of the yearly recruitment into the British army was Irish due to the low pay and the struggle of the majority to survive.

The army's main role in this so-called peacetime was acting in aid of the civil power such as escorting prisoners, protecting sub-sheriffs executing judgements against defaulting tenants and tithe payers, to keep the peace at fairs and to search the country for arms. Nothing much has changed to this present day in Ireland.

HEALTH

The landlords, being the local gentry, were the people who the British Government instructed to provide for the social and health needs of the poor. This policy was doomed to failure from the beginning and the British Government were forced to step in and build 600 dispensaries throughout the country and by 1835 ten special asylums were completed.

PUBLIC WORKS

By 1845, with millions unemployed, loans and grants of about £1,000,000 were allotted to build canals and roads which was known as 'Relief Works'. However, this sum was only a drop in the ocean of what was required to avert starvation of the millions of poor.

EDUCATION

In 1823 the total numbers of elementary schools in Ireland were 36,490, Protestant 21,000, Catholic 15,300. During the period 1745 – 1832 the total state grants came to £1,000,000. At the Synod of Bishops at Thurles held in 1850 the Archbishop of Armagh, Paul Cullen, after his recent visit to Rome, debated the role of the Catholic Church and the State in Irish education and with the State handover to the bishops as a result, the start of our present problems commenced.

POVERTY

The report of 1836 on the scale of poverty in Ireland which shows the number of people who were unemployed for over a half year was 600,000. Add dependants and the total was at least two million. The problem was said to lie with the excess population and the scarcity of capital.

By 1841 there were thirty-seven workhouses in operation which housed 30,000 people. By the end of that year close on 100,000 wretched poor were sheltering in those homes.

It became clear at an early stage that the schemes adopted by the government – organized emigration, road works and land drainage by their own would not relieve the appalling suffering of the millions of starving people. It is said that the British used those schemes as a smoke-screen to hide their true intentions which were to eliminate most of the Irish race, when one examines this period, bearing in mind that the Establishment had clear warnings from previous mini-famines. Excuses such as bad management, the failure of the landlords to do their duty, middle-men and so forth are not acceptable reasons for the holocaust on such a large scale, for Britain had at this time full control by her laws and administration to rule Ireland.

My conclusion on this matter, and many would agree, is that Britain be brought before the World Court of Justice to answer for her policy and actions in Ireland in this period. The historians, too, have a lot of explaining to do, for they kicked for touch on all matters relating to the holocaust but sided with the Establishment when required.

INDUSTRY

By mid 1836 the railways had come to Ireland and by 1850 up to 1,300 miles of railway were in use. At the same time about two million pounds were spent building the Grand Canal. The landlord owned all the land but was not obliged to fund any of the social schemes or invest, in the short or long term, for the well being of the people and country. Yet, as we see here before, the British Government were relying totally on the landlord for investments in what they termed the Free Market conditions. As a result, Irish industry could not compete with Britain and even less with the imports from America, in particular grain imports.

AGRICULTURE

It is estimated that the population in Ireland had reached eight million by 1841. With industry being wiped out by the Free Market, the people depended on agriculture for employment. With rents for the tenant farmers greatly increased as land became scarce vast numbers of the population depended on the potato crops. The beginning of the end was at hand for the Irish race. I believe, as others do, that there were enough food-stuffs in the country to accommodate at least eighteen million people.

EMIGRATION

With the decline in industry and the landlords' control of agriculture, hundreds of thousands of people had no work. Emigration policy was now the cure. Between 1780 and 1845 over one and a half million emigrated to the U.S.A. and Canada, the vast majority to the United States. As Canada was a British Colony, emigration to Britain from 1831 – 1841 is estimated to be 450,000. Frederick Engles' description of the Irish in Britain in 1844, was, I quote, 'Little Ireland Ghetto In Manchester.'

TOWN AND COUNTRY

In 1841 two-thirds of the population lived in rural areas of the countryside. The resident landlord, living in the big house, also owned the adjoining town or village or both and was the king of society at the same time over forty per cent of the houses (if you could call them houses). They were more like cabins, with earth floors, roof made of sod of earth laid on timber rafters and covered with thatch material, no windows, no chimney, walls made of mud and all had only one room. As thousands starved the Catholic Establishment was in the middle of a huge church building programme throughout the country.

TRAVEL IN IRELAND

It is estimated prior to the holocaust that up to one hundred thousand people were using the canals every year. By the middle of 1845 the stage coach service of Charles Bianconi covered over 3,000 miles every day by means of up to one hundred cars for a fare of 1½d. per mile. This would seem to be a great achievement at that period.

LANGUAGE

In 1800 half of the population, it is said, spoke Irish. By 1851 only a quarter spoke the Irish language.

The main reason for the collapse of the Irish was that both Maynooth and the Catholic Establishment used English as the language of the pulpit as English was the law in the land. The Church, being Britain's agent in Ireland, could not offend her master or go without the perks and power for the sake of the Irish language.

REPEAL PHASE 1 AND 2

It is said that Daniel O'Connell was the greatest single political force in Ireland in the years 1830 – 1848. In order to become a full time politician he gave up his practice at the Bar and in return he received about £16,000 per year from 1830 – 1847 from a special collection called O'Connells Tribute. Both repeals failed even though he had the full support of the Catholic bishops.

With the country, in 1831, in a state of crisis, the soldiers and police were engaged full-time protecting the Establishment from proctors, process-servers and keeping the law at tithe seizures and auctions. At Newtownbarry seventeen were killed at a tithe auction when a magistrate gave an order to fire on the crowd.

THE HOLOCAUST

In 1847 the potato crop had totally failed again and with it went the main diet of the majority of the people. The worst affected areas were the south-west, west and north-west and the census figures of 1851 clearly show the results.

The population statistics between 1841 and 1851 show a twenty-five per cent decrease. Emigration would account for one and a half million, famine deaths would make up the other one million.

Emigration for 1849 – 1852 was around 250,000 yearly made up of small farmers, labourers and the wretched poor.

The full suffering of the people is best summed up by a Cork magistrates (a man of the Establishment who at all times would be putting the best side of the position) by his visit to Skibbereen in West County Cork in December 1846. I quote, 'I entered some of the hovels or cabins no tongue or pen can convey the appearance of the dying, dead, skeletons, four children, a woman and what had once been a man'. Even today those words bring a chill to the heart.

RELIEF

Question: were the measures taken by the British Government to relieve the social impact of the potato failure responsible for the holocaust? John Mitchel indicted the British on a clear policy of genocidal intent. Others say it was a natural disaster, an act of God. I claim that the British, as Government for Ireland, had, or should have had, all information and facts regarding the events leading up to the holocaust and, therefore, I agree with Mitchel's answer to the question. And, as already stated, Britain should be tried for alleged mass murder and other crimes against the Irish race.

To say that British policy in Ireland before and during the holocaust was not genocidal is to 'call the kettle black face'. The sight of ships leaving ports all over the country, full of grain and other products, for England and elsewhere, while in Ireland thousands were dying of starvation, provoked deep and bitter anger particularly as the country was self-sufficient in food-stuffs.

18

CHAPTER 5

WHEN IRELAND STARVED

The following is based on a T.V. Radharc programme, *Why Ireland Starved*.

The miserable living conditions in Ireland, have been compared with North America whose misery was abject. Worthington's survey, in 1846, concluded that nothing could compare with the bog-holes of Ireland.

In 1845 John Bull's account caused great anxiety in England, they had conquered Ireland several times, the population was almost extinguished – yet they survived, the problem was that British policy on Ireland was made uncertain by English politics.

In 1663 the amendment of Irish Law by England forbade exports of Irish goods to Europe unless the goods first went though English ports.

In 1665 the export of Irish cattle to England was forbidden. The Irish in turn bred sheep instead, then the English prohibited the export of wool. The penalty for noncompliance was a £500 fine, and as a result many jobs were lost.

In 1691 the English refused to allow Irish Catholics to be educated abroad. Noncompliance with this law meant expulsion to the West Indies.

On the death of a Catholic their land was confiscated and handed over to a landlord (in most cases a Protestant) and, in due course, their sons would own all the land.

The Catholics were persecuted on grounds of religion. In other words, the minority persecuting the majority. With no industrial employment, access to land was a matter of life and death.

In 1759 restrictions by law on the importation of cattle resulted in evictions being the order of the day. The Irish acknowledged the landlord's right under English law to deal with his people. Rents increased up to six-fold under penalty of eviction.

In 1746 the English stopped the export of Irish glass and the *import* of glass to Ireland except from England. They stopped the export of cotton and silk. The result of all this was that Ireland could not compete with the growth in England under such conditions.

In 1840 the land per acre (conacre) rose to £10.00 per acre and land which was not viable was auctioned. The only option for the masses was to improve the land but the rents were too high and they were forced to emigrate or starve. Confiscation of land was now widespread. The Irish lived by the whim of their landlords and any disrespect of them resulted in immediate eviction. All rent returns (all wealth was extracted from all over Ireland) went to Britain, part being returned for the benefit of the landlords' villages, towns and the big houses.

The Church of Ireland, being the official Church, stole from the poor, in rent called tithes, £600,000 per year and, in order for the landlords to get their share of the tithes, the British Government enacted a new law so they could now collect by adding the tithes to the penal rents. This income was not spent to help the Irish poor but on appointments of bishops as favours to the English, for out of a total of twenty bishops only two were Irish.

The year 1842 found six million pounds in rents and goods drained from Ireland into Britain while the Irish starved.

In 1835 the Poor Law inquiry found three-quarters of the population were unemployed. The Irish economy was used by the British Establishment to generate the supply of cheap grain and other products for the British market. Even at this time the town of Westport, County Mayo, was very wealthy. Then came the decline with the Industrial Revolution in Britain and again she passed laws to inhibit production in Ireland. Then came the start of the famine which made it an even bigger disaster due to the lack of industrial alternatives.

In 1841 the social life of the masses was such that they had plenty of turf to keep warm, especially in the west of Ireland. The Irish married young on the advice of the bishops, so they might help each other in times of stress.

The average plot of land for each family was half of one acre per year, and the population had reached over eight million.

1845 The Duke of Wellington (Arthur Wellesley) wrote of the tragedy in Ireland. Ireland's starvation was the result of the evils of the British government. There were plenty of provisions of food-stuffs available but that did not matter for the masses had little or no money with which to buy food.

The merchants, who could foresee the coming disaster, appealed to the Government for help. They were told that public money could not be spent on the on-coming famine and on 15th August 19845, turned a blind eye to the announcement that the potato blight had arrived.

In 1846 the reports of the James Mahony and Harringlass inquiry found in Skibbereen, County Cork, shanty houses of poverty, funerals every day, fever rampant, people just waiting in pain to die, four dead for six days, bodies eaten by dogs. In February alone 3,700 died here of hunger. The Government blamed the landlords — Lord Carberry collected £15,000 rents on his estates which Skibbereen and the surrounding areas were part of. The winter of 1846 – 1847 was the worst, and most people died in or around the workhouses.

WORKHOUSES

'No medicine, no food, no drink, no fire', was the finding of the C. J. Russell Inquiry in Bantry. In County Cork along, 4,000 died in April 1847. Sliding coffins were used for the first time in order they could be re-used. The verdict of an inquest held in Skibbereen at this time was Wilful Murder *on the part of the British Government.*

On 31st August 1847 people marched on Captain Perceval's estate in County Sligo begging for food and work. He politely told them he had done all he could do and that there was nothing further he could do. The outdoor relief programme amounted to only £50,000 in total where as fifty million would not have been enough. The British Establishment knew by not providing the necessary funds they would be getting rid of at least one million poor by starving them to death. As one British official said 'one million is not enough'.

Lord Clarenden, Lieutenant-General of Ireland, said the population of

Ireland is decimated and Lord John Russell demanded that no food be imported to help the starving Irish. Like Sligo, the same conditions applied to Counties Mayo, Galway, Donegal. Leitrim and Clare.

In 1848 – 1849 it is estimated that close on one million poor were in the workhouses, places of last resort before dying. Those places could not cope with the number seeking admission and the price paid by the poor for the disease-ridden buildings was that they had to give up their heritage. A Mr. Killean paid £4.00 per acre per year for land. He owed no rent but he lost everything and, forced to go to the workhouse to die, his home, like all others and villages, was knocked down so that the landlord would not have to take care of him or pay the rent. At this time in Kilrush, County Clare, 7,000 people died of hunger, being the entire population of the town — and again all of the houses were pulled down in order that the landlords could take over the property and get rid of the people who wanted the houses for shelter.

In order to be admitted to the workhouses the people had first to give up their land. The workhouses were financed half by the British Government and half by local rates. As most people had no money it meant no rates, so the workhouses had to close down and the people who had signed away their land to be admitted had now no place to live.

In 1844 the figures show it cost £1.00 to collect one shilling in rates and tenants with land valued at £4.00 could not afford to pay. The landlords were thus given the excuse and the power by the British Government to evict their tenants and so avoid being rated.

Soup kitchens provided the cheap way of feeding the masses, with the Society of Friends as the best group to provide the service.

In Dungarvan port at this time riots broke out when the people saw Irish food being exported. Trevelyan, the British agent, employed up to two thousand soldiers to keep order. Ireland, prior to the great famine, had enough food for up to ten million people. The British blamed the cause of the famine on 'God's Providence'.

By 1846 up to 85,000 poor of the west of Ireland, most of them evicted from their homes by the landlords, were forced to emigrate to North America from small ports in Sligo, Mayo and Galway.

The Irish peasants were just pawns used by their British colonial masters and the landlords over the rent issue with each blaming the other for the misery and suffering of the Irish people. Others would view this account as being too generous to the Establishment and would say that the Irish people were victims of a colonial system which sought to ensure that 'John Bull's other island could never be a threat to England'. They would be happy to see the Irish race eliminated for good. This hardship, misery, hunger and death that occurred to so many on such a large scale was never before, or after, witnessed in the history of the planet.

The foregoing is just a short note on what happened and why Ireland starved. I will be raising some of these points again later in the book.

CHAPTER 6

IRELAND'S GREAT HUNGER
1845 – 1850

The following is based on Cecil Woodham Smith's book *The Great Hunger 1845 – 1849.*

There is little doubt that by 1845 Britain became more concerned with the threat from Ireland than any time since 1169. Over a period of seven hundred years Ireland had been conquered many times, the land being confiscated. After the Cromwellian victories only about half a million Irish survived and yet the Irish nation still existed, separate and hostile. Not even the Act of Union in January 1801 changed the hostility.

The Union, it is said, was to be a marriage for the benefit of the two Kingdoms, but it turned out to be a Brutal Rape, for Britain used Ireland as an easy market for her goods. Daniel O'Connell is quoted as saying his admiration for Queen Victoria 'The darling little Queen of Ireland'.

By 1844 Britain had more soldiers in Ireland than she had in India because the hostilities were so bad between the two countries and had been since the Reformation of 1600. Ireland, right down through the centuries from 1600, used England's difficulties for her opportunities and in every crisis the Irish used her weakness to demand their right to freedom.

The conditions in Ireland prior to the great famine were found by the French journalist Beaumont as 'Worse than the Negro in chains' and the German Kohl said that 'the poor in Europe had a life of comforts compared to the poverty and misery of the Irish'.

In 1841 the Duke of Wellington, a man of the Pale, wrote 'A country in which poverty existed to the extent it exists in Ireland, with housing conditions where the wretched poor sought shelter is beyond words'.

In 1837 the village of Tullahobaghy, County Donegal, with a population of 9,000 had but ten beds, ninety-three chairs and 240 stools in it. The people who were evicted and the poor unemployed made shelter by putting sods over ditches, banks and lived in bog-holes, yet by 1847 six million pounds in rents were transfused from the Irish poor into Britain.

In 1835 a British economist, Nassau Senior, informed the Government that up to two and a half million Irish were unemployed for almost eight months of every year. At least ten families were existing on one acre of land due to the high price of the land and sub-divisions were on a large scale. Anyone who had this amount of land had hope, not starvation.

By early 1846 the Government debated the Ejectment Bill in the House of Commons. This piece of legislation empowered the resident and absentee landlords to evict families at will from the land. This left the people on the roadsides. They wandered from place to place, dispersed by police and soldiers at the whim of the local landlords. Death on the roads and lanes and death in the ditches was the result.

One member of the House of Commons commented – this power to the landlords 'is tantamount to a sentence of death by slow torture on the Irish'.

The west of Ireland's sub-divisions systems or, as it was known by the locals, the 'Rundale' system, was rented common divided in such a way that tenants got a mixture of land some good, some bad and in many different areas. One County Donegal man had his land in over forty separate places and with the large increase in rents he was forced to give it up. The rents were now a hundred times higher in Ireland than in Britain.

The 1845 Devon Commission Report on Ireland on the eve of the great famine warned the British Government in grave terms of the dangerous state of the country. The British dismissed the report and warnings by saying it did not contain anything new that they did not know about. Their minds had already been made up that their policy for the property of Ireland must support the poverty in Ireland and the menace of the Irish to Britain be removed.

Again in 1845, Sir James Graham's (Home Secretary) report of his inquiry into the state of the Irish crop said a failure in Ireland would be a disaster and Gladstone wrote 'Ireland, Ireland, that cloud in the west, that coming storm'.

On 15th October 1845 the British Prime Minister, Sir Robert Peel, decided to repeal the Corn Laws but his Bill was defeated on the vote in the House of Commons. The British Establishment were more concerned to protect their farmers, free trade and, of course, private enterprise than help an under-developed country. This British policy on Ireland was bound to end in tragedy.

Robert Peel had at least six years' experience in Ireland prior to becoming Prime Minister. As Chief Secretary in Ireland he had full knowledge of what was happening in Ireland and how British policy affected the country on the eve of the great famine. It should also be remembered that it was British policy in Ireland when the nineteen previous smaller famines from 1727 – 1844 occurred.

In 1846 the Relief Commission for Ireland was put under the control of Charles Ed. Trevelyan with the official title of Assistant Secretary. He had complete power and control and his influence with the House of Commons members allowed him to administer the Poor Law Relief in Ireland as he saw fit without any interference. The Poor Law Commission's report of 1846 states that up to two and a half million people were starving every year whether the potato crop failed or not. This report, when taken in conjunction with Nassau Senior's report of 1835, would confirm the proof of John Mitchel's statement that British policy was of clear genocidal intent on the Irish people.

In February 1846 the British again brought the 'Coercion Act' into law in Ireland. This was the eighteenth of such acts to come into force since the Act of Union. It gave the British Government, landlords and soldiers Martial Powers to do as they pleased with the Irish without having to answer to anybody. As William Smith O'Brien said, the British Government sent no food but soldiers – Ireland was to starve and be coerced.

As the great famine approached the evictions also increased; three hundred tenants on Mrs. Gerrand's Ballinglass, County Galway estate on 13th March 1846 were evicted with the help of the police and soldiers in order that all the cabins could be demolished and all the holdings turned over to grazing farms. None of the tenants owed the landlords any rents, but at their own expense and hard labour had reclaimed the land from a bog. The evicted tenants slept in the ruins of the cabins for the first night, but next day they were driven out to live in a hole in the ground two to three feet deep, roofed over with sticks, turf and sods of earth, for no neighbour was allowed by Martial Law to give them shelter of any kind.

In April 1845 the British Government were aware that the £100,000 they spent on Indian corn-meal from America to replace the total loss of the potato crop valued at £3,500,000 would result in the deaths of thousands of people by starvation before the new crop was ready to eat in August at the earliest. To add to the problem, the majority of the three million starving could not afford the high cost of the Indian corn.

Robert Peel's advice on this matter to members at the House of Commons was, 'But if it is known that we undertook to supply the Irish with food we would to a great extent lose the support of the Irish gentry, landlords and Irish clergy. It is quite impossible for the British Government to supply up to four million people.' Yet at this time and throughout the great famine years, wrote John Mitchel, 'Ireland was producing sufficient food, wool and flax to feed and clothe not nine but eighteen million people. Yet a ship sailing into an Irish port during the famine years with a cargo of grain was sure to meet six ships sailing out with similar cargo.'

Figures produced in the British House of Commons up to February 1846 confirm Mitchel's statement. Modern Irish and English historians treat the figures with caution. They say corn grown in Ireland before the great famine was not sufficient to feed the people; they also say that during this period four times as much wheat and Indian corn was imported than exported.

It has been clearly established here before that, whatever is the correct figure, and I agree with Mitchel and others, the vast majority of the Irish people could not afford the high cost of the essential food stuffs and whatever small amount of money they had went to pay the high rents. To quote Sir Randolph Routh, Chief Officer in Ireland for relief to Charles Trevelyan in January 1846, 'it would be a desperate man who ate up his rent with the certainty before him of eviction and death by slow torture.' The Irish poor were furious to see food protected by the soldiers exported from Waterford after arriving from Carrig-On-Suir. It was a sight which the Irish people found impossible to understand and impossible to forget.

In August 1846 when it became clear that the potato crop was a total failure from Donegal to Cork, from Galway to Dublin, on 2nd September *The Times* declared 'Total Annihilation' of the Irish people and once more the question was asked what would the British Government do to save Ireland.

On 20th August 1846 *The Times* reported that there was not even a loaf of bread or milk to be got in County Longford and this applied to people who had money to pay for it. Sir Randolph Routh wrote to Charles Trevelyan who wrote back instructing Routh that the leftovers or crumbs of biscuits at military stores be given out, otherwise the British Government was not prepared to supply food. But they were ready to call out the troops to contain the starving masses.

On 31st August Captain Perceval wrote of 'The subjection of the masses at Westport, County Mayo'. A large and orderly body of people, many of respectable families, marched on Westport House to see Lord Sligo. When the lord came out someone cried 'kneel, kneel', and the crowd knelt down before him. He told the crowd there was nothing he could do for them. In the late autumn of 1846 with the general harvest a total disaster in Ireland and a part failed in Europe, the British Government made no adjustment to their policy on Ireland. Except in some areas of the west, everything was left to private enterprise. By now all Indian corn in America was bought up in full by the Europeans. The only corn available was the 'floating cargoes' on the way to Europe. Sir Randolph went to London to see Charles Trevelyan and Charles Wood at the Treasury. He told them that private enterprise will not help the starving Irish. Trevelyan told him that some of the 'floating cargoes' would be diverted to Ireland providing the price of the corn was right. He was too late. The winter had arrived, shipping was dangerous, and supplies would not reach Britain until the late spring of 1847.

The Commissariat Officers serving on the Irish Relief declared that the British Establishment knew, but cared more about their overseas colonies than they cared about Ireland.

The chairman of the Devon Commission, Lord Devon, in October 1846 said that about four thousand men in his neighbourhood had no work and were starving and were daily around his house demanding relief work, which as yet had not been started by the Board of Works. People in Rossbercon outside Newross, County Wexford, were starving and in a wretched state; at Mallow, County Cork, around 200 men forced their way into the workhouse rather than receive a rate of 7d. per day on outdoor relief; such a rate would not prevent them from dying of hunger.

On 3rd September, Charles Trevelyan wrote to Sir Randolph – 'Do not encourage the idea of prohibiting exports, perfect free trade is the right course.' Ireland starved.

The conditions of the 1845 relief schemes were such that no work on drainage or other related works could be done since landowners boarding off the scheme would have their property improved and increased in value, while other land owners whose land was further away would get no benefit. The rules stated – no person in the area could profit more than another, so roadworks was the only scheme available at 7d. per day and in most cases the roads were good and no extra work was necessary.

By 1st October 1846 all vegetable and potatoes were gone, yet the British Government insisted that the starving poor pay high prices for the small amount of food available. This problem was very bad in County Cork, where the Indian corn from America was almost used up. The amount left could not be eaten until it was ground and this had to be done in Britain for there were no corn mills in Ireland.

On 12th November 1846 Charles Trevelyan wrote again to Sir Randolph in Ireland – 'All we can aim to do is distribute the existing stock of food at current prices, if however. the people have no money to buy the food, those must be placed on charity'. How this was to be carried out with up to four million starving he did not say. Denis McKennedy died on 24th October 1846 when working the road scheme in Carberry, County Cork. He had received no pay since 10th October. A post-mortem by Dr. Donovan and Dr. Due certified death as a result of starvation. There was no food in his stomach or in the intestines. The verdict of the coroners court inquest was that he died of starvation caused by gross neglect of the Board of Relief.

The winter had now set in, and the hundreds of wretched human beings, whose appearance resembled scarecrows, had combed the potato fields and existed on nettles, blackberries and cabbage leaves until all was gone.

By 3rd November more than half of the children in the workhouse at Skibbereen, County Cork had died since the 1st October. Lord Monteagle appealed to Sir ruth to open the food depots, he refused by saying, 'We can obtain no effort until the parties are subjected to a little pressure'. To make matters worse the weather turned very cold with six inches of snow and drifts in County Tyrone as early as 12th November. It would seem that nature had joined with Britain as the enemy of Ireland for the winter of 1846 – 1847 was most severe and the longest in living memory. In England the River Thames was iced over.

By the end of November many died on the roadworks from starvation. The people had become bewildered as the British Government made no attempt to help, but treated them with contempt.

By 16th December 1846 hundreds of people slept in ditches and doorways, wrote Fr. Matthew. They begged for food and shelter but were driven away by the police. In Cork alone one hundred people died each week from starvation. Many of those who died were employed on the public works schemes. The 7d. per day rate of pay could not begin to buy food for a family, even if that food were available.

There were by now some 300,000 on such schemes and due to the lack of organization and dishonest supervision the system broke down with the result that both men and women who had worked on the schemes while their land lay idle were expected by the British Government to stay alive without food until next year's harvest while they tilled their bit of ground.

On 15th December 1846 a propaganda report at the behest of the British reported that up to 30,000 pieces of arms were purchased by the Irish poor from Birmingham, England, in order to rise up against the British. This propaganda was used for the purpose of excusing Britain from being responsible for the starvation in Ireland. But, as the manuscript of James Hack Juke dated 4th January 1847 observed, even if the report were true that the poor were arming to fight, in their present physical condition, they would not have the power left in them to use such arms.

By the end of December 1846 most of the public works schemes had closed down. Charles Trevelyan wrote to Sir Randolph on 8th December – 'We have reached an important crisis in our operations in Ireland's future prospects'. Things were so appalling the British Government was shortly going to be faced with the alternative of letting the Irish starve or of feeding them out of the public purse.

By 24th December 1846 the crisis was so bad that Captain Wynne on a visit to Clare Abbey wrote to both Colonel Jones of the Board of Works and to Charles Trevelyan explaining the crisis as he found it in County Clare, when he saw the extent of the starving among women and children. Mothers half-naked, shivering in the snow and sleet, their children screaming with hunger. 'I am a match for anything else I may meet with here, seeing this I cannot stand', he wrote. The public works at Clare Abbey re-opened on 28th December 1846 as a result.

The outcome of the British Government's famine policy in Ireland in December 1846 with particular reference to Charles Trevelyan's letter of 8th December to Sir Randolph, was to let the Irish starve. This decision by the British not to provide food is best highlighted in Skibbereen, Co. Cork, when on 15th December the magistrate of Cork, Nicholas Cummins, paid a visit to Skibbereen. He wrote to Lord Duke Wellington and a copy to *The Times* who published it on 24th December 1846. Part of the contents are as follows, and I quote: 'Being aware that I should witness scenes of frightful hunger I brought some bread, the village was deserted. I entered some of the hovels to find the cause and the scenes which I saw were such as no tongue or pen can convey the slightest idea of. In the first six hovels famished or ghostly skeletons to all appearances dead were huddled in a corner in filthy straw. I approached with horror and found by a low moaning they were alive, they were in fever, four children, a woman and what had once been a man. It is impossible to go through the detail, suffice it to say that in a few minutes I was surrounded by at least 200 such phantoms, such frightful spectrums as no words can describe either from famine or from fever, their yells are still ringing in my ears and their horrible images are fixed upon my brain.'

The conditions as described were confirmed in full by the British Commissariat officer Richard Inglis when he visited the area on 17th December 1846. The British Government's reaction to the starving in Skibbereen – Charles Trevelyan issued instructions to all landlords in the district to contribute to the relief but no emergency supply of food was sent to Skibbereen. Much the same conditions applied in Killarney and Tarbert, County Kerry and in County Leitrim. Captain Layard, Board of Works Inspector, reported cart-loads of orphans, whose parents had died of starvation, were refused admission to the workhouse. Fr. John O'Sullivan, parish priest of Kenmare, Co. Kerry, found a room full of dead people and a cat was eating one of the dead children. Commander

Caffyn of H.M. Steam Sloop *Scourge* wrote the following to Charles Trevelyan on 15th March 1847: 'On discharging a cargo of meal for the Society of Friends at Skull off the west coast, out of a population of 1800 three-quarters of the population were skeletons and were starving to death. At Ballinakill 150 people were dying of the same cause and if the Board of Works Relief is stopped thousands will die. In Ennis, Co. Clare conditions were so bad that 1200 men were starving as a result of the relief works closing down, one man described the scene, "Nothing to do but bar the door, lie down and die".'

In March 1847 William Bennett described the type of fever which now struck the starving, known as 'Famine Dropsey', a horrible disease resulting from long continued famine and very low living in which the limbs and then the body swell and finally burst. The existence of this fever epidemic was undeniable throughout the country yet the British Government would only accept that it occurred in a few cases. Also, In March the Central Board of Health received reports on the workhouses in Cork, Bantry and Lurgan where many people were in a deplorable state and dying at the rate of one per hour. In Cavan, Ballina, Kenturk, County Cork, Sligo, Newport, Co. Mayo, mass graves were dug near all workhouses for mass burials.

The Irish dreaded the workhouse and the fever hospital because so many died there. In Ennis, County Clare, far fewer died who were not in the workhouse or hospital, whereas in Tralee, County Kerry, people who sought shelter and help in those places contracted the fever. Thousands preferred to die in their own homes.

With the total failure of the potato crop of 1846 and widespread fever the Irish now had no option but to leave Ireland and in a mass movement they made their way to Canada, but mostly America. They took the disease with them to a new life of suffering.

The mass movement of people leaving in 1846-1847 in the hundreds of thousands because of starvation is one of the most important and historic events of world history. It is said by some that there was great joy in the British Establishment because their sought for elimination of the poor Irish was now being accomplished voluntarily by the Irish themselves.

The forced emigration of about one million in the period 1845 – 1847 to America achieved very little but caused great hardship, misery and hunger. It took a second or third generation of emigrants to achieve any success and power.

With the timber trade from America to Europe booming at this time, the British used the emigrants as ballast on the outward journey from British ports to America at low fares in order to fill the ships and make a nice profit and at the same time get rid of the Irish race.

The population of U.S.A. at this time was twenty three million and British Canada only 1,000,000. Most of the Irish emigrants used the low fares to Canada as a means of getting to the U.S.A. as the Irish looked to America for refuge and a life for their children.

The Irish in the U.S.A. felt that freedom for them was not in British Canada and they had had enough of British rule.

In February 1847 Charles Trevelyan wrote that all roads to the ports in Ireland were thronged with Irish people heading for ships to emigrate. One Board of Works official reported a list of people on the works as useless, they had all gone or were dead. Most of the Irish emigrants at this time travelled to Liverpool and then to Canada. All ships with emigrants who came up the St. Lawrence River had to stop at Grosse Island quarantine station some thirty miles down river for medical inspection. Those ships with fever on board were detained and the sick taken to the quarantine station hospital. I will be mentioning Grosse Island many times more in this section and again elsewhere to bring home to the reader the frightful pain, suffering, torture and death that the Irish emigrant had to endure on this island in particular, also, the dedicated courage and bravery of staff who risked their lives to help comfort the sick and dying.

In 1847 the St. Lawrence River was late opening to shipping due to the long and severe winter. When the first ship *The Syria* arrived on 17th May the ice was one inch thick as reported by the *Quebec Gazette*. It had eight-four people with fever on board out of a total of 240 emigrants, nine had died on the high seas and one died when unloading at Grosse Island. *The Larch* ship from Sligo sailed with 440 emigrants of whom 198 died at sea and 150 arrived at the quarantine station with fever. *The Virginus* sailed from Liverpool for Canada with 476 of which 158 died at sea and a further 106, including most of the crew, were sick when landed. This ship had taken extra weeks to make the crossing, the suffering of even the healthy emigrants was appalling reported Dr.

Douglas, the appointed superintendent of the quarantine station hospital in Grosse Island by the British Canadian Government. He wrote – the few people that were able to come up on deck of the ship were ghostly yellow looking spectres, unshaven and hollow cheeked. The worst emigrant ships were the ones which brought the landlords' tenants to British Canada and of all the suffering endured in Ireland during the Famine years nothing could compare to the hatred felt around Ireland or left behind by the forced emigrants as 'the landlord emigrants'.

In January 1847 the British Government announced in their policy that the whole destitute population was to be transferred to the Poor Law much the same as had happened in England, Scotland and Wales for some time past. This Poor Law for Ireland was to be financed out of local rates at the expense of property owners in Ireland only. With the landlords as the only owners of property they set out to reduce the number of tenants on their estates. In most cases this was to avoid the increase in rates. In the rest, it was in order to stay solvent.

In order for the British Government to remedy the world-wide bad publicity of their policy of evictions they connived with the landlords of Ireland in a policy of forced (not voluntary) emigration as an alternative. The British Government's own emigration agent, Mr. Perley at St. John New Brunswick in British Canada, denounced Sir Robert Gore-Booth, a resident landlord, for 'exporting and shovelling out the helpless' to the detriment of the colony. In reply Sir Robert put forward the landlords' point of view, declaring that forced emigration was the only humane method to put the country on a satisfactory footing. The country, he went on, was over-populated and to emigrate was the only solution. Emigration also saved money by as much as fifty per cent on each emigrant and no doubt the British were delighted with the results. Now they had the emigrant to slave in another of their colonies to enhance their power and fortune and at the same time were able to woo public opinion at home and world-wide to their humane and generous treatment of their Irish subjects.

Nine ships left County Sligo with 2,000 emigrants from Lord Palmerston's Estate and arrived at Grosse Island in a deplorable state. Almost all were naked, many were sick and many had died on the journey. There were scenes of diseased dying daily and left on the Montreal wharves with little or no help. Many who did help the sick died themselves of fever as a result, men like six Catholic priests, Right Rev. Hudon, Vicar-General to the Bishop of Montreal, Dr. Power, Catholic Bishop of Toronto and John Mills, Mayor of Montreal who died in November 1847,

The Victoria Bridge and railway sidings now replace the sides of the sheds which housed the stricken Irish emigrants at Point St. Charles, Montreal. At the entrance to the bridge there is a large shrine on which is inscribed: 'To preserve from desecration the remains of 6,000 emigrants who died from ship fever AD 1847 – 1848.'

On 30th October 1847 the Grosse Isle quarantine station hospital closed down. In the wooded valley, one of the most beautiful valleys of Grosse Isle, the site of the emigrant cemetery, a four-sided monument commemorates those who died. The inscription reads 'In this secluded spot lie the mortal remains of 5,294 persons who fleeing from pestilence and famine in Ireland in the year 1847 found in British Canada but a grave'.

There is a second monument on Grosse Isle, a Celtic Cross of granite on which are three inscriptions in French, English and Irish:

Thousands of the children of the Gael were lost on this island while fleeing from foreign tyrannical laws and an artificial famine in the years 1847 – 1848.
God Bless Them, God Save Ireland.

Of the hundred thousand emigrants who sailed for British Canada in 1847 it is reported that by the end of the year 20,000 had died, 5,300 at Grosse Isle, 17,000 in Quebec, Montreal, Kingston and Toronto and 1,120 died in the Province of New Brunwich and 25,000 at least were in hospitals. It is estimated that up to 20,000 perished crossing the Atlantic from hunger and fever.

A U.S.A. Commissioner for emigration wrote: 'The whole route of the emigrant ships from Europe to North America would long since have assumed the appearance of a crowded cemetery.'

Due to strict regulations imposed by the United States Emigration Office no major disaster occurred as a result of famine emigration. All ships with fever and starvation were turned away, as was the British Brig. *Seraph* from Co. Cork to Boston with 118 cases of fever on board.

Likewise the Brig. *Mary* also from Co. Cork was refused and had to go to Halifax, Canada, with additional misery, suffering and death of the emigrants on 17th June 1847.

The United States quarantine station was located on Staten Isle for the sick emigrants most of whom were Irish. The conditions afforded to the Irish in New York were no better than in British Canada. The housing was horrific and the emigrants lived in cellars underground, in rat infested rooms, whole families in one room. With high rents charges for such slums anything better was beyond the means of most emigrants.

The position of the thousands of starving who fled to Britain in 1847 is best summed up by the British Government, 'Ireland should be compelled to provide for its own people'. The majority of the landlords were now bankrupt and used as scape-goats by the British when they transferred the cost of the Poor Law in Ireland to local rates on the property owners.

In 1847 it was said by the British Government that they failed to understand why the Irish of the west coast of Ireland did not use the good supply of fish. If they had taken the trouble to find out the explanation was very clear. The boats which they used were not sufficient for the sea conditions which together with the hazards of the coast, made regular fishing difficult. The weather also meant that fishermen could not go to sea for weeks and had to rely on public works to buy food until such time as weather permitted them to fish.

By October 1847 there was further bad news for the starving Irish. With a financial crisis in Britain, the railway and grain shares collapsed, and any relief for Ireland was now gone. Charles Wood told Clarenden, 'I have no money' and refused to help.

The Union of Ballina covered some half a million acres, with a population of 120,000 people. On the 12th June 1847 some 260 of them, starving and destitute, walked from Erris to the gates of Ballina workhouse. They were refused admission as the place was full. In any case, as the rates in their district were not paid, they would not be admitted.

There were some 130 unions covering all Ireland, most by this time were on the point of collapse with Ballina and Westport, County Mayo, being the worst affected. So a repeat of the British Government's neglect of 1845-1846 continued at the expense of the starving millions. With the failure of the landlords to pay the higher rates their tenants were now being evicted on a massive scale and the British Government's response to the crimes committed in their name, 'let the starving Irish fend for themselves'.

On 24th December 1847 a Major Halliday, Poor Law Inspector, reported that people were starving in the Sligo workhouse and the coroner's verdict was that the deaths were due to starvation. 'To see such sights of suffering and wasted humans, I cannot wash them away from my imagination.' With yet another winter at hand, the main concern of the British Government was with Clarenden's report to Lord John Russell of the increasing discontent, of hatred of British rule in Ireland, and the alarming number of assassinations of landlords over the past couple of months. He wrote, 'There never was so open or so widely extended a conspiracy for shooting landlords and agents and my fear is, this will spread and the flames which now rage in certain districts will become country wide.' He was convinced that the murders were part of a general rebellion campaign. The intention, he told Sir George Grey, is to shoot landlords and agents this winter, drive away all the resident gentry from the country, and make the management of property so dangerous that the occupiers will be able to keep possession.'

On 20th December 1847 the British moved on Law and Order (to hell with the starving). They passed the Crime and Outrage Ireland Bill. Under this Act the Lord-Lieutenant of Ireland was given dictatorial powers. To meet the threatened rebellion he could suspend all rights and introduce Draconian laws at will. As 1847 ended and 1848 began, with the workhouses full and people dying of starvation inside and outside them, with rates impossible to collect, employment non-existent and fever as never before, Ireland's final fate was awaited.

The repeal movement was now the only power left in Ireland, but at this critical time the officials of the movements turned their backs on the terrible conditions caused by the famine and became absorbed in Party Politics. The result was that the Young Ireland Party in July 1846 left the association because they refused to pledge themselves never to resort to armed force and rebellion as Daniel O'Connell and the bishops wanted. The leaders of the Young Irelanders were William Smith O'Brien a Protestant landlord and a member of the British House of Commons, Charles Gavan Duffy, Thomas Francis Meagher, John Mitchel and

Fintain Lawlor. Both Mitchel and Lawlor were in favour of a Peasant War, a guerrilla war.

On 18th March 1848 Francis Meagher wrote in the nation's newspapers, 'if the Government of Ireland insists upon being a government of dragoons and bombardiers, of detectives and light infantry, then up with the barricades and invoke this God of Battles.' Meantime famine was still raging the country, with the west of Ireland the worst, the workhouses full and the jails overflowing.

By the summer of 1848 the British had brought into Dublin an extra 10,000 soldiers and had all the leaders of the Young Irelanders arrested. John Mitchel's trial was swift and he was brought into the dock at Green Street Court-house by the underground passage, and found guilty of sedition and sentenced to fourteen years in Australia.

On 22nd July 1848 another Bill was passed by the British suspending Habeas Corpus in Ireland until March 1849. As a result all members of the Young Irelanders were open to arrest or rebellion. It was clear that the people were not in a position for war due to there being no arms and the continuing famine. The only place where the 1848 Rising took place was near Ballingarry, Co. Tipperary, on Saturday 30th July at McCormack's farmhouse. It was a minor affair and a failure.

The shadow of yet another fearful catastrophe covered Ireland. The potato blight, as before, appeared all over the country and there was every sign that a total failure of the crop had occurred again.

On 16th July 1849 the blight had spread country-wide with Skull, Castletown, Galway, Carlow, Birr, Mayo, Sligo, Limerick being the worst affected.

Charles Trevelyan wrote on 19th July: 'But we are in the hands of providence, without a possibility of averting the catastrophe, if it is to happen we can only await the result.'

The complete loss of the potato crop had, yet again, its effect on the starving people. To make matters worse the landlords were heading for bankruptcy and to sell their estates in the present conditions in Ireland would be very difficult. On 30th August 1949 *The Times* reported that due to the attempt at rebellion, the British had decided to go slow on relief in Ireland and let the Irish go down on their knees and beg their masters for help.

During the period of August to December 1848 in Kilrush, County

Clare alone, 6,090 people had been evicted and by 22nd January 1849 880 more were turned on to the road bringing the total for less than six months to 7,000. It continued at the rate of 150 people a week and likewise the same applied all over the west of Ireland.

Captain Kennedy (later Sir Arthur Kennedy) wrote of his experiences on the famine in Ireland: 'I can tell my Lord (to Lord Carnarvon) that there were days in the western country when I came back from some scenes of evictions so maddened by the sight of hunger and misery I had seen in the day's work that I felt desperate to take the gun from behind my door and shoot the first landlord I meet.'

On 30th September 1849 Charles Trevelyan informed Twistition that Treasury grants to the distressed Irish unions were to cease for the Chancellor of the Exchequer had said there was no money. With all other funding gone, with despair and ruin now sweeping the country, those who could get the money together made arrangements to begin a new round of emigration.

On 30th October 1848 Lord Mounteagle gave examples of the type of new emigrant – farmers of good class who could afford the fare. One man had thirty acres, had paid all his rent, had put up good buildings and a house on the farm. Likewise, in Meath, Sligo and Cork, all were heading for the ports of Dublin and Cork in their thousands. Charles Wood wrote to Lord Mounteagle, 'I am not at all appalled by your tenantry going – that seems to me to be a necessary part of the procedure.'

In the large Ballina Union thousands of acres looked as if they had been devastated by the enemy. In Erris seventy-eight townlands were without a single inhabitant or a four-footed beast. In Munster it was the same with large tracts of arable land deserted or squatted on by paupers living in huts or ditches. Lord Monteagle wrote on 3rd November to Lord John Russell, 'We shall be left in a warren...' The Queen was patron of the largest union workhouse the world has ever built.

Ireland of 1849 was now at the mercy of Charles Trevelyan's policy of natural causes. On 9th February Clarenden told Prime Minister John Russell that he was unable to shake the opinion of Charles Wood or Charles Trevelyan that the right course was to do nothing for Ireland and leave things to the mercy of natural causes. The official British line to the world would be that no deaths due to starvation would be allowed to occur in Ireland. But, in private, their attitude was different as Benjamin

Jowett the Master of Balliol said, 'since I heard one of them say that he feared the famine of 1848 would not kill more than one million people and that would scarcely be enough to do much good...' The man he referred to was the British Government's political and economics affairs adviser, Nassau Senior.

In order for the people to get food they were forced into crime, the jails were full. As a Mr. Shaughnessy, a traveller, pointed out: 'I am satisfied that they had no alternative but starvation or commit crime.' He found the young people as he travelled from town to town, were almost naked with hair standing on end and eyes sunken, bones of the little joints visible, he asked himself, 'Am I in a civilized country and a part of the British Empire?'

On 9th April 1849 Lord Monteagle estimated that up to sixty unions were on the verge of closure and he was astonished to find some of those were in Leinster and Ulster. It was, he wrote, a new frightful picture and by English standards the whole of Ireland was in ruins, dilapidated and starving.

In March 1849 an epidemic of cholera broke out to add to the suffering and left the starving people with little or no relief. Sympathy for Ireland had gone. Her misfortunes had been too frequent, too hopeless and too impossible to remedy. Censorship had killed all compassion. By June of 1849 even the Quakers, who had done so much to help over all the famine years, gave up relieving the Irish. But the British had one last policy to cheer up the starving and to distract the people from the suffering – Lord Clarenden's tonic – Ireland was to receive a visit from Queen Victoria.

On 2nd August 1849 the Queen and Prince Albert arrived in Cork to a welcome of bonfires. It is said the Queen and the Irish people fell in love with each other for a brief period. On their arrival in Dublin on 6th August the Queen wrote, 'The scene was wonderful, striking never to be forgotten'. At the same time she wrote, 'The poverty of Ireland did not escape me, you see more ragged and wretched people here than I ever saw anywhere else.'

The papers reported that the visit was a great success. However, for the starving Irish the hunger continued in Ireland. In 1879 there was another potato failure and reports published deplored the state of Ireland in words which might have been written in 1846.

The British Government's policy in Ireland at all times was described as genocide — race murder. It is also said they had no plans to destroy the Irish nation and that the government's only crime was their inability to foresee the consequences. Sydney Smith wrote, 'The English seem to bid adieu to common feeling, common prudence and common sense the moment the very name of Ireland is mentioned.'

To me it's very clear why no official firm figures exist of deaths by starvation in the period 1845 – 1849. The census of 1841 shows a population in Ireland of over eight million. In 1851 the census showed six and a half million. The Census Commissioners calculated that, at the normal rate of birth increase, the total population should have been more than nine million over this period. This would show that two and a half million people had died of starvation or were forced to emigrate. It was in the interest of the British Government not to record deaths by starvation so as to avoid being answerable for their crimes against the Irish people.

In order to show that the great hunger was not confined to the west, south-west and north-west there is the following written by Elizabeth Smith wife of Colonel Smith, landlord and magistrate near Blessington, County Wicklow, 'the signs of the coming great famine is very evident in 1842 in Blessington'.

On 5th April 1848, 'Colonel Browne knew all the members of the United Irishmen by his detective police who bring him accruable information so that the poor fools are all in the net and will be dragged to light when the fit moment comes.'

On 12th November 1849, 'things so bad all are off to America and we miss them not.'

On 21st January 1849, 'there are 1300 people in the workhouse here and crowds are turned away for want of room.'

On 24th February 1850, 'God help the people the roads are beset with tattered skeletons.'

If this was the state of things within the Pale of Ireland can anyone be expected to apprehend the conditions, suffering, misery and starvation which were allowed west of the Shannon and in Munster for years, prior, during and after the great famine?

CHAPTER 7

THE FLIGHT OF THE IRISH
TO CANADA FROM FAMINE

I mentioned before The Act of Union which became law in 1800. Ireland was to be ruled directly from London from then on. Dr. Samuel Johnson pointed out earlier, 'Do not make a union with us, we should unite with you only to rob you!' The first complete records kept from 1825 – 1845 show a half million Irish arrived in Canada alone.

In 1847, at the height of the Holocaust, at least 20,000 Irish refugees died on ships and at quarantine stations at Partridge Isle, New Brunswick, in towns and lands of Quebec and Ontario. As many as ninety per cent died at the Grosse Isle quarantine station hospital in the most deplorable conditions. It is only in the recent past that Canadian writers began to tell the story of the Irish-Canadians who were treated worst than slaves. Maguire (whose name I will be coming back to later) stated that for most of the Irish refugees it would have been better for them to have stayed in Ireland and died at home. The hardship, misery and suffering caused to so many, even at an early period, showed how the British Establishment and their Canadian Colony censored all information. They used black propaganda to highlight the very few success stories to give the world at large the impression that they were doing their best for the Irish people.

In 1823 Peter Robinson, a Canadian, and a British emigration agent, arranged with eight major landlords in Ireland covering Munster and Connaught to take fifteen hundred workers off their estates to be transported to new townships in the Ottawa Valley of Canada, with the blessing of the Catholic bishops of Ireland.

Some of the landlords involved were Lord Kingston with his 100,000 acres estates in Donerach, Mount Cashel and Ennismore. Sir William Wrixon Becker of Ballgiblin House, Colonel Jephson of Mallow, Captain Robert of Charlesville and Richard Aldworth of Ennismore his son-in-law, who lived at Newmarket, Co. Clarel.

By the end of May 1834, A.C. Buchanan reported, at Quebec City a total of seventeen shipwrecks had been recorded. Fr. E. J. Horan, volunteer at Grosse Isle quarantine station hospital, wrote that the shortage of food is the principle cause of all the sickness and death and half the people who arrived from Liverpool, England and Cork in Ireland in 1847 were almost dead from starvation.

On 2nd July 1847 there were almost one thousand people sick in quarantine at Partridge Isle and 350 at Middle Isle near Chetham.

On 11th and 12th July four ships anchored at Grosse Isle had 4,000 sick and 340 had died at sea. At Grosse Isle at this time 2,500 emigrants were in the quarantine hospital.

Irish emigration was not natural, but artificial, since the poverty of Ireland was produced by Britain and emigration was not social but political and the majority of the exiles knew they were victims of the declared British policy.

Some writers in collusion with the British Establishment, and others as stated before, would like us to believe that most of the seven million who went to North America up to 1922 went voluntarily. I refuse to accept this explanation, for the facts speak for themselves.

It is argued that the Irish were poorer in 1844 than they were in 1691 due to the full market forces applied and the contempt by the British for the well being of the Irish people. As one visitor explained, the Irish have to furnish England and her colonies with vast amounts of food-stuffs for the want of which they themselves are starving.

A landlord in Ireland, by the end of the seventeenth century, could scarcely invent an order which a servant labourer or butler dared to refuse to do. Nothing satisfied him more than unlimited submission and there is little use in going to law with the devil while the court is held in hell.

In 1786 the Catholic Bishop of Munster removed two of his priests whose conduct and arrogance had made them especially obnoxious to their congregation.

By the end of the 1800s the parish priests had assumed, virtually unchallenged, authority over the lives and thoughts of their congregation and Ireland had the most clerically repressed Catholic peoples in the world. This was accomplished with the help of the landlords and the British Government, for a handful of landlords in each county of Ireland were owners of all the land. Lord Antrim, for example, owned a 173,000 acre estate.

In 1834, H.D. Inglis, a British visitor, reported that most tenants could not pay the rents without limiting their diet within the bounds prescribed by the necessities of nature, especially in Munster and west of the Shannon.

In 1836 new legislation and other repressive rules against the poor Irish made the landlord responsible for the evictions and emigration. British troops helped them to reinforce the law.

The ships carrying the Irish emigrants were known as the coffin ships and these were not confined to the famine period alone. As far back as 1800 twenty-five per cent of the exiles died on those floating prisons. In 1845 Charles Trevelyan was more convinced that Ireland's great evil was not famine but selfishness and that charity might be more demoralizing to the Irish than the starvation that was killing them. Sir Robert Peel, Prime Minister, helped somewhat but Lord John Russell, Peel's successor, ignored the holocaust.

Between 1845 and 1855 one and a half million people emigrated to U.S.A., 340,000 to British Canada and about 300,000 to England. In all about 2.1 million or one-third of the Irish population emigrated in just eleven years. In this period, more emigrated than over the previous 250 years.

In 1848, the British newspapers and a wide selection of journalists reported the naked truth of the British Government's policy of systematic extermination and recolonization of Ireland that they had chosen the great famine of 1847 to be the final act to achieve their policy.

Sir Thomas Wise, a Catholic landlord and leader of Catholic emancipation, urged the completion of Ireland's regeneration by financing mass emigration. He was supported in this by Archbishop Cullen who feared there would be civil disorder and destruction of all things religious which his clergy would be unable to deal with.

From 1845 to 1855 the Irish population fell from 8.5 million to 6 million as a result of starvation and emigration. From 1856 to 1921

Ireland lost 4.5 million with about 3.5 emigrated to U.S.A., all in the name of The Free Market. What a human holocaust forced on the people — to achieve progress, we are told.

Between 1848 and 1855 the average number of evictions per year was 10,000. In 1882 there were 27,000 people evicted and between 1876 and 1886 132,000 suffered the same fate. As Karl Marx had prophesied 'the entire Island's true destiny that of an English sheep walk and cattle pasture'.

It is estimated that over seven million Irish emigrated to North America between 1600 and 1921; ninety-five per cent went to the United States of America.

The United States of America, unlike British Canada, escaped the worst of the famine holocaust by their strict emigration regulations. By turning away ships with the sick and dying in 1847 they used Ellis Isle as a quarantine station hospital.

It is said that 1847 was the worst episode of human misery in Canadian history. In 1897 being the fiftieth year after the holocaust, a Mr. Gallagher, a relative of one of the famine victims, visited Grosse Isle and set about to clean up the graves which had been neglected and, on the 5th August 1909, hundreds attended a service for the unveiling of a Celtic Cross. As for Partridge Isle and all the other quarantine stations where the Irish starved and died there is no record of any monuments erected to honour the dead.

At this time Britain had 50,000 soldiers in Ireland to maintain law and order. The cost was greater than the total cost of the United States army and navy combined. As a result, most of the so-called financial relief for Ireland went on the army of occupation.

The winter of 1848 – 1849 was just as bad as 1847. Landlords evicted in their thousands. In County Wexford the suffering was not as bad due to the organization of schemes adopted to distribute the available food to the people in the greatest need. However, in the period 1845 – 1852, there were up to a 1000 in the workhouse built to house only 600 and many died from starvation. The evictions in the County were a lot less than, say, Kilrush, County Clare, and most of them occurred in the north of the County.

In the paupers' graveyard, Coolcotts, Wexford, a Celtic Cross was erected to honour the dead who were buried here in mass graves between

1852 and 1939 with the inscription: 'In this place known only to God, Lie the bodies of Wexford's poor, suffered handicapped and destitute'. Remember them.

On the question of voluntary or involuntary emigration one has to take into account the ancient culture and traditions of the Irish people. The market economy, forced on the country by the British Government, at a time when agriculture was the single biggest source of livelihood for a population of nearly 9,000,000, meant that the only alternative to emigration was death by starvation. In this regard the British Establishment with their many allies connived to bring starvation and emigration about. In the final analysis, the question comes down to this, did the English, and later from 1800, all British Governments cause the most horrendous and inhuman crimes against the Irish people and their property with no redress to Natural Law and Natural Rights?

The writer has made quite clear, in other sections of this book, the answer to this question and I will leave it to the readers to make up their own minds. Of the estimated 100,000 who emigrated to Canada by force in 1847 some 25,000 of them died on ships, quarantine stations and in the country-side within six months of landing in Canada.

CHAPTER 8

AN EXPERIENCE OF THE EMIGRANT, 1847, TO BRITISH CANADA

This is a true story of one man's experience and bravery as an emigrant to Canada in 1847, I quote from Gerald Keegan's own journal:

February 18th 1847: Due to the conditions of the people in County Sligo and I being one of two thousand tenants on Lord Palmerston's huge estate and being the village schoolmaster I am in a better position to gauge the conditions and misery of the people than most, the plight of the children was very sad due to hunger and neglect, no people anywhere in the world should be reduced to the level that the people of Ireland had to endure this day when thousands of tons of the best food are being shipped out of the country under armed guard from every port daily.

February 19th: I had some friends call to see me about emigration, they claim the whole country is on the move in mass emigration to Canada a forced expulsion plan conceived and executed by the landlords with the connivance of the British Government.

February 20th: the landlords wished to get rid from the vast estates the helpless, starving, disease-ridden tenants and in a panic situation the poor people are easy victims and most of them are in no condition to emigrate.

February 21st: the potato famine affected the whole country but the west, north-west and south were the worst areas affected, but there were plenty of corn, wheat, meat and dairy products, but the tenant would be liable for prison, even execution if they put their hands on any of this.

February 22nd: the numbers attending school are dwindling every day and soon a decision will have to be made to tell the children to stay at home and close the school.

February 25th: with a few friends and a couple of newspapers there is a picture of reality of these dark days when deprived of the necessities of life human beings are known to become predators, killing and robbing others so that they may survive.

February 24th: The school closed today, after mass on Sunday the Proctor got up on a stone in front of the Church and announced that the landlord had taken the desperate situation of the people into consideration and said there is no hope for you in Ireland, if you leave and go to Canada, rent in arrears will be cancelled that is due. Passage to Canada will be paid and a tithe to free land. Marriage in those conditions to Eileen would be out of the question.

February 26th: As the school children had a week off, a visit to Connemara and Galway confirmed the intensity of the suffering along the west coast with thousands dying, some were dead with grass in their mouth, dogs, donkeys have become a common item of diet, I made plans and inquired about emigration to Canada for it now seemed that the landlords had banded together to rid the estates, as the people had no longer the strength to till the land and are no longer useful to their overlords.

February 28th: The people had but one week to make a decision on emigration and it was now becoming clear the nature of the deal, the leaders of the Young Ireland group were opposed to the crooked deal and a large number of the people joined this group, the London Times was still against us and by their propaganda blamed the Irish people for the state of the country.

March 1st: by now most parts of the west and south people had got tickets for Canada and dates for sailing were posted. Some relief of corn from United States was promised and local relief grants but most of the latter ended up on the pockets of the greedy corrupt officials.

March 3rd: school started after Christmas with 23 pupils, this week there were 14 left.

March 7th: went to Church, met some of my old friends and discussed the state of the people. The southern report published in Cork was given to me by Father Tom O'Hara it read as follows; A large steamer *Ajax* which sailed yesterday from Cork consisted of 1514 firkens of butter, 102 cashs of pork, 144 hogshead of whisky, 844 sacks of oats, 247 sacks of wheat, 106 bales of bacon, 13 bales of ham, 145 cashs of port, 12 sacks of vetch, 28 bales of feathers, 3 cashs of magnesia, 8 sacks of lard, 296 boxes of eggs, 30 heads of cattle, 90 pigs, 220 lambs, 34 calves and 69 assorted packets and the same time hundreds of families at Baltinglass, Co. Galway were evicted from their homes.

March 9th: In County Cork two boys aged twelve and fourteen were transported to Australia for seven years for stealing some corn, the town of Westport, County Mayo was a fearful sight, the poorhouses were full, the Claddagh fishermen had to sell their nets and tackle to buy soup and corn. It would seem ninety per cent of the people were in the poorhouses or dead in the district.

March 10th: There was no shortage of recruits to join the Young Ireland Movement, no effort was made to arrest the enlisted men for the same reason as was the case in all previous uprisings, but to wait until the movement had reached the stage to strike, all the leaders were arrested. [See also page 39 chapter 6.]

March 11th: The school will close for good tomorrow therefore final decisions on emigration will be made tomorrow night.

March 12th: All the good-byes were made to the school children, March 25th is the choice for the wedding date. The landlords had selected the old, the infirm, the children and the destitute for the first shipload to Canada. All able to work were held back on the estates for production. The British convinced the Pope that we are an nation of secret societies and in revolt against the laws of the land, excommunication is the result.

March 13th: Too little too late the world outside began to hear of the Irish people's plight and sent money, the most important donation received was from a small tribe of North American Indians, The Chocktaw.

March 14th: A riot occurred in Limerick yesterday some of the Young Ireland Groups attacked a food convoy on the way to a loading port, hundreds of troops marched on them, many were shot down others arrested.

March 15th: Public auction in the village, to be sould by publick cent one pit of property of widow Scott, one pettycoate and one apron the property of the widow Galaher seized under and by virtue of an order for the tythe due to Rev. John Boolsides.

March 16th: The eviction squad were today smashing down the house of a dying woman.

March 18th: The children looked like old people, no laughter and play anymore, thousands were now ready to emigrate and no mention of the ten shillings for each when arrived in Canada in the legal document which everyone had to sign or else.

March 20th: Next Thursday is the wedding day Fr. Dan Flynn will perform the celebrations as Fr. O'Hara had been sent out of the country by the bishop, or he would have been tried for treason.

March 22nd: Eileen's father died, he had to be buried at once, the funeral was arranged for tomorrow.

March 23rd: Uncle Jeremiah brought the body of Patrick on a horse cart to the graveyard, there were just three of us present.

March 24th: Tomorrow is the big day all the neighbours were preparing for the wedding feast.

March 27th: Thursday was the big day and everyone had plenty to eat and drink with a dance and ballads afterwards.

March 28th: No Church service today, Fr. Flynn is down with the fever, this is the last Sunday before leaving to catch a boat. All the tenants had signed the papers and were told to be in Dublin on 2nd April for embarkation.

March 30th: We are on our way it will be close to get to Dublin on time, there are delays of a week or more so to make sure that the ship is full.

March 31st: We now joined a huge army forced to leave their native land for the convenience of the rich and the powerful.

April 3rd: We stayed overnight in Ardagh, County Longford. There was hardly any room on the roads with the number of people on the March, many died and all the people had to shelter in the open and were not allowed to board ship to protect themselves.

April 5th: Dublin is not spared from hunger and disease and in some cases are just as bad as the west coast, Cholera is the biggest cause of deaths in the country and Dublin is no different. It takes 36 to

80 days for the crossing.

April 6th: Four of the would-be emigrants died during the night. One little child died from exposure, no help from the shipping office for the sick, [that was common practice during 1832 emigration, some ships had left days late so that they were loaded in full with human ballast for the benefit of the chartered purse].

April 7th: Still waiting for order to board ship with Eileen doing a great job attending to the sick.

April 8th: Several men tried to get on ship last night but they were beaten back for if once on board they are entitled to food rations, so the ship owners make sure that the passengers embark only at the last minute, permission was finally given to board ship today, when the ship had moved into Dublin Bay it stopped, the crew would not sail on a Friday, being superstitious.

April 9th: The *Naparinra* being the name of our boat sailed at daybreak, it had accommodation for three hundred, but five hundred were on board and the captain gets £5.00 for each passenger. Three days of rations and sea biscuits were served of which most were eaten on the first day as the people were starving with hunger, half of the passengers had no place to bed down for the night, the holds are dark, no light, no portholes and no ventilation, fresh air was by means of two hatchways and width for each passenger is only half the legal allowance of 33 inches. As we sailed along the east coast we could see Wicklow and County Wexford and we were close to Carnsore Point, finally the hills of Kerry faded out of sight, We all said farewell to our beautiful Country with tears in our eyes.

April 10th: This evening we faced a choppy sea, we were getting our first taste of the violent Atlantic, the rolling and creaking of the ship in the storm was frightening, how the people will survive for six or eight weeks when it's so bad after only two days, with conditions down below the stench from the refuse and excreta was sickening, the sick were huddled on the floor in a sea of water, Eileen and I got to our bunk and I settle down to read the first part of my journal, the sea calmed some by early morning.

April 11th: As this day was calmer many of the people were able to go up on deck, many were sick and over one hundred were unable to move, Eileen and I went below the visit the sick and helping as much as we could, the only food been served is sea biscuits, there are a rare treat of tea, most have some of the food we brought on board.

April 12th: We had another bad storm this afternoon with mountainous waves, only the healthiest survived the storm without bodily harm, the weak and the sick had a painful time of it, Eileen found some cases which may be ship fever.

April 13th: We all had a dreadful night last night, no-one got a sleep, it was a wonder the *Naparinra* didn't fall apart with the force of the wind and the waves. We tried to get down to the hold this morning but the emergency hatch was stuck so we couldn't open it. In the afternoon with the storm abating the ship's mate ordered the hatches to be opened to let the people up on deck. Aunt Mary was very ill with high fever and with conditions in the hold she could not last long, one old man was lying on a bunk with several ribs broken, there were no services or ship's surgeon on board. A ten year old girl died during the storm, we wrapped her in some rags and slipped her body into the ocean in silent prayer. The captain was informed that fever was on board, 'You Lie' he said.

April 14th: Aunt Mary is holding on, the only crew member who ever dares to go down below is the steward, he do so in order to collect sixpence from anyone who will buy a drink. It's hard to blame a person for taking a drink to help blot out the awful reality of living in a place what is not fit for animals to live in and since the captain and the mate share the profits on any whisky sold there is no way it can be controlled.

April 15th: I am now pleased that I continued the journal on the ocean so that the conditions which the Irish emigrants are forced to travel may be brought before the public, the Canadian Press may be able to highlight the facts on ship and what is going on in Ireland.

April 16th: Three elderly women helped themselves to a huge teapot full of tea and over a fire on deck they keep it hot. All on board got a taste.

April 17th: it was the loveliest day so far, down below the fever is spreading like wildfire, the sick are becoming indifferent to the punishment they are taking, they are losing hope, we try and get them up on deck.

April 18th: Aunt Mary died this morning, we slipped her body into the Atlantic, we keep the family with us on deck all day. The outbreak of fever is causing panic among the passengers and crew, this afternoon I got a pan of stirabout for some sick children, you can get anything if you pay enough. A man jumped overboard, we helped his daughter who was on board with him.

April 20th: Several burials had taken place during the night, food is getting scarce and with the fever spreading it seems now that none of us can escape it. We had some snow this evening, the weather is very cold, I counted five bodies tossed overboard this afternoon.

April 26th: Eileen was ill for the past two days her medicine box is now empty, the mate refused any of the ship's medicine and said he is not running a hospital.

May 4th: We have spent four weeks on ship, today I had a fight with the mate after he had beaten Tommy who was doing chores on deck, I gave the passengers a bit of excitement.

May 7th: We passed through large ice fields yesterday and great skill is required to avoid a collision. More ocean burials again which is now a common sight, I reviewed the journal this evening and feel pleased of what it said to date.

May 9th: They say at least 20,000 perished on the ocean. We were told this morning that we may reach Canadian quarantine station in two weeks, the St. Lawrence River is a hazard and demands skill. Sunday on board, we tried to get as many as possible on deck for service.

May 12th: Both Eileen and I spent some time every day down below helping the sick, preparing bodies for burial. We were lashed all day yesterday with strong north-west wind, we got a good number up on deck today, we were informed we are approaching a big shoal of fish.

May 13th: We had a good day's fishing all on board had their fill.

May 14th: The drinking water had now become another crisis, it's so filthy it's dangerous to use. After six weeks on the Atlantic we've seen our first flock of birds and the passengers were in high spirits.

May 16th: On deck this morning I see land on both sides, Cape North and St. Paul's Island and lighthouses were in view, everyone got excited.

May 18th: Mrs. Finnegan died today. We had reached the Gulf of St. Lawrence River and all who were able were on deck to see the beauty of it.

May 19th: As we sailed up river the traffic is getting to be dangerous, the 'Mingan Rocks' were the scene of many tragedies and great care have to be taken by the captain and crew.

May 20th: We were early to be boarded by a river pilot, a Frenchman, we dropped anchor, the pilot said the fog is too dense in this area to continue.

May 21st: The scenery is great this day, our ship is the only thing out of harmony with nature. There had been at least three burials each day for the last week and the fever is getting worse. It's sad as we are so near our destination.

May 22nd: Progress upriver is very slow, the scenery continue to be beautiful with dotted small white coloured farmhouses on the south shore, four other ships at the other side of the river were waiting like ourselves for the tide to turn. At midday two men approached from the shore with items to sell, but on seeing our boat and conditions of the passengers they were not keen to come aboard, I paid the men five shillings for a pail of milk and three loaves of bread by rope to ship.

May 23rd: The Landscape continues to be a feast for the eyes. We got most of the passengers on deck to enjoy the show and help them to forget the dark and sorrowful days and nights that we have gone through.

Deckhand Martin Riley told us today one ship crashed on the 'Mingan Rocks' a few days ago over three hundred were lost. We were also informed that dozens of emigrant ships had departed mainly from Dublin, Cork and Liverpool in late March and early April with Ireland's leading export of human beings.

May 24th: The mate is still keeping a close watch on me, I am certain he will square the account with me before our final parting. We had a surprise today, fresh water as the ship's supply is like sewage. We sighted bodies floating in the river which is becoming a common sight now, yesterday we had five deaths. We hope to keep the bodies on board now as we are so near our destination, the boatswain said it might take three or four more days due to the slow progress of the river. We remained at anchor all day today, the *Naparinra* was motionless. There were five more deaths today. In spite of all our efforts, conditions in the hold remain filthy and the fever is out of control. All hands of the crew were now engaged in putting the ship into best trim, scrubbing, painting, to be ready for the inspection officers at the quarantine station, so that the *Naparinra* can go ahead with its human trade, the appearance of the decks now belies the conditions of the passengers quarters down below where no inspector will go.

May 25th: The wind has changed so we are on our way and may land soon, we have been over seven weeks confined to this floating tub but as some emigrant boats took up to twelve weeks to reach the end of the journey we can count ourselves lucky. As I write this note I hear the anchor being weighed. Everyone was excited this evening.

May 26th: We went on deck early this morning, the country church bell was announcing an early mass. The most amazing sight of all is the number of ships ahead of us, behind us and all round us, all at anchor, like the *Naparinra* they too are in shipshape for inspection, the last one of the group is Grosse Isle. We are due to be inspected, those who do not have the fever will go to Quebec. I am making this entry in the early afternoon as we may be at quarantine this evening, Eileen is packing our few belongings in case we change boats, four more died this morning, for about four hundred down below there is no excitement as they are lying in their bunks unable to move. Timmy came rushing with the news that we are in sight of Grosse Isle, this may be my last note on board.

May 27th: They were in no hurry getting us on board when we left Ireland and now they appear to be in no hurry getting us landed. Last night the *Naparinra* weighed anchor off Grosse Isle and hoisted her ensign as a signal for the inspecting officers. We could have a long wait unless there is a large number of inspectors as there are thirty to forty other boats anchored in the river. After waiting all day a medical officer boarded our ship all passengers who were able to stand up were marched by him, those who showed signs of infection were herded into a group together with the ones down below to be landed at the quarantine hospital. We waited for further developments, I took this time to write this note in my journal, whether or not I will write any more I do not know at this time, I have told in my own simple way the story of how the poor have been treated in my country, my only regret is the limitations that words have in my attempt to use them to express the depths of misery to which thousands have been reduced by famine and persecution.

The final blow for all to be driven from our land and transported in the holds of the most dilapidated ships in the world to a foreign land, I have merely touched the surface of a massive tragedy. If this is the end of my story I hope that it contains enough of the truth to let the world know how sorely we have been tried by the tribulations we have endured.

May 28th: We had to remain on the *Naparinra* overnight, it could be due to the swarm of boats already at the dock, sometimes I am told there are delays of several days awaiting orders to land the sick, I got my journal out again to relate on the days events.

The general appearance of the quarantine station, the land dock is in a disgraceful condition with broken planks and unsteady supports, most surprising is two large sheds with bunks not far from the landing area, surely this is not the Canadian quarantine hospital. It looks as if all the bunks are occupied, it seems to be a very primitive looking quarantine station. Eileen came to tell me they are lowering the boats to bring the sick ashore. We hope to be in Quebec by tonight to end our honeymoon.

June 2nd: After four days and five nights of confusion and mental anguish I take up my journal again. The mate finally got even with me, while transporting the sick to shore we had to rush them from deck into the boats and leave them lying on the dock, we removed seven dead bodies in one boat, back at the dock I got a shock for Eileen was standing among the sick waiting on me, why are you looking at me so? I have come as you requested she said, looking out to the river I saw *Naparinra* had slipped anchor and was heading for Quebec, the mate won the last round of the fight.

June 3rd: The frightful conditions on this island caused me immense anxiety in seeing Eileen being exposed to. We both used a lean-to for the moment as a place of shelter with some straw and covered with a blanket to sleep at night. A loaf of bread and some tea for two shillings, Eileen may be getting the fever she is not eating.

June 4th: Today Eileen was unable to move, I could not get a doctor until late evening, he gave me a note to get medicine at the hospital.

June 8th: After the last few dreadful days and nights I went through I have the heart the pick up the journal again, Eileen is dead and I am all alone. For three days I had watched as she went through spasms of racking pain and raging fever in and out of delirious. This afternoon with bursting heart I knelt by her as life ebbed out of her, I looked for help, a Fr. McGoran came and said prayers for my dear departed, he told me she would have to be buried without delay. The burial place was a field where the dead tossed six deep in trenches, we agreed to dig a grave in a secret spot at north side of the Island hidden behind trees, nothing in the world could induce me to leave this island now, its earth encloses all that I hold dear in the world.

June 9th: This morning Fr. McGoran brought me a bite to eat, I thought I was having a dream but the grave reminded me it's a reality. I began to help out with the hundreds of sick who are getting no attention as a result of shortages of doctors, nurses and attendants in general.

June 10th: I awoke early today after a small amount of sleep, Fr. Tom O'Hara called, he had been sent by the Bishop to avoid arrest at home, I spent an hour at Eileen's grave today, tomorrow I will start to help the sick. The fever sheds are a fearful sight, all day long I can hear the cries and moaning of the fever patients.

June 11th: I am determined to keep my journal up to date right to the end whatever that may be for I am sure the outside world know nothing about this final act of our tragedy on this lonely island.

June 12th: At noon today I had tea and biscuits with Fr. McGoran and two young french priests, they and the doctors are the heroes in this mass tragedy. I spent most of the day with tears in my eyes seeing the misery, illness, hunger and neglect. There is an endless line of ships out in the harbour today. The quarantine station is already overcrowded, today they begin to put up tents to take some of the overflow, it is incredible that the Canadian Government is not taking emergency measures, but as like Ireland, Canada is ruled by Britain and what can we expect.

June 13th: Today Sunday no time to rest work to be done. I met Uncle Jeremiah and the two girls Ellen and Bridget they are in poor condition, like many of the bunks theirs was filthy, too sick to do anything for themselves. The quarantine Island is a disgusting place, beside the sad symphony of cries of pain and mental anguish in the fever sheds day and night we can hear the daily harvest collection of the grim reaper, it's the sound of little wagons as they haul the dead to the west end of the island where the burial trenches are located they take up to ten bodies each trip, on a bad day the amount of dead can be over one hundred. Yesterday we counted thirty seven ships out in the harbour, some drop two or three hundred at quarantine and this is only a fraction of the ghost fleet, at this rate thousands of the victims will end up in the burial trenches, many has escaped from the fever sheds only to drop dead among the bushes in remote areas of the island.

June 14th: On my way to visit Eileen's grave this evening, Fr. McGoran came along and invited me to take a walk around the island. It appears to be about one mile wide by two miles long, it's a natural paradise and man has made a temporary hell out of it, my friend told me he visited a ship yesterday, every side lay the dead and dying, it was barely five feet high, the filth and foul air add to the tragedy.

June 15th: During the day my work takes my mind off the feeling of loneliness that grips me during the night and with Eileen gone the feeling is much worse. I am able to put up to eighteen hours a day helping the sick and dying with hundreds of patients who are just lying in their berths without any attention being received. The crowding and the filth are almost as bad as on the ships, the berths are in tiers so that the people in the lower ones are targets for whatever waste and excreta fall from above. The dead are removed only at certain fixed hours with the result that the living often have to lie for hours beside a corpse.

The government had several warnings about the hopeless inadequacy of the facilities here, even now this state of emergency nothing is being done, as an example of how desperate the situation is they have to open jails in Quebec to get helpers. If it were not for the courageous band of volunteers such as the Anglican Catholic churchmen and doctors the situation would have been a lot worse.

June 17th: There is one ship that has been out in the harbour for a week with all passengers still on board, two priests went out to visit it and reported eleven dead in the hold and the crew were paid to slip them into the river at night time. Dr. Douglas told us he send a delegation to the government in Montreal a week ago, but was told they had more urgent matters to deal with. He warned them they must not heed alarmists who he said were giving too much publicity to the Grosse Isle affair.

June 18th: On being told that another shipload of emigrants from Sligo was in the Harbour I and Fr. O'Hara went to see how the passengers faired, dead bodies were being loaded by the dozen into boats by sailors who were paid one sovereign each body brought to shore. The conditions of this boat were even worse than on the *Naparinra*, the captain done all he could to help the passengers, his load of emigrants were from the north-east section of Lord Palmerston's estate where they lived in extreme poverty where famine and fever claimed many victims.

The number of patients on the island has doubled in the past two weeks but no increase in supplies coming in from Quebec. A steamship the first one I've ever seen stopped in the harbour today to pick up passengers from the shore it looked as if about a thousand were crowded onto the decks, Fr. McGoran told me that the trip to Montreal was even worse than the ocean crossing, the passengers are left two days without shelter or food, many reach Montreal more dead than alive.

On my way to watch at Eileen's grave today I found the body of a man in the thicket nearby, he had crawled there away from the horrible sights and sounds of the fever sheds to die in peace.

I am spending part of my sleepless nights adding to this little account of what looks like the final act in the mass tragedy of this summer of sorrow.

June 19th: I fear that they will have to send another military unit to control the company of guards who are already here, their conduct is becoming increasingly unruly, the Island would be much better off without them. It is now estimated that there are over two thousand now in the fever sheds.

June 20th: Several of the clergy and many of the doctors have come down with the fever, I feel my own turn will come for I have been very close to the sources of contagion for a long time, I got permission to look after the little herd of cattle and some repair work for a break from the patients which I was glad to do.

June 23rd: I awoke from a pitiful sleep this morning with every bone in my body aching. Dr. Douglas came, gave me some medicine, and to stay in bed, the medicine eased my suffering enough to allow me to pick up my journal once again, I had a compelling urge to continue telling my story as long as I am able to write, if they move me to the fever sheds it will likely be the end of it all, this could happen tonight or tomorrow.

June 24th: I stayed in my cot all day, Fr. McGoran suggested I receive the last rites which I agreed to. The mental anguish of the past two weeks was replaced with the feeling of tranquillity in spite of the racking pains of the fever, there is much more to be written but every effort is painful and my writing is getting illegible.

June 25th: After a very bad night I improved a bit around noon today, had a cup of tea and some broth, but the fever picked up again this evening. The most distressing of all the symptoms is a very disagreeable odour which develops in the late stages of the fever, this applies in my case now, this signals the end Dr. Fenwick's expression that it's too late now for medicine.

This evening I asked Fr. O'Hara to look after this little book, and my few belongings for I don't think I will be able to write anymore, I am leaving in it the address of my Uncle Dan O'Connor who lives in Montreal, I also left a note with my cousins Eileen and Bridget telling them how to get to my Uncle Dan.

This writing looks very shaky. In reverent memory of all who have perished in this holocaust and of all who have suffered in any way as well as to all those who have spent themselves in a heroic effort to help us, I dedicate the message in this little book.

Farewell, Gerald Keegan.

June 27th: Closing of the journal, I Fr. Tom O'Hara am adding the following notes to my dear young friend's journal at his request, he is still alive I don't think he will last long, I spent almost all night reading the journal through, I feel like Gerald that it is urgent for the world to know about what is going on, it is probably the only weapon we have. The little book is a treasure of factual information, its only defect as Gerald wrote, is that it falls short of the full reality of the depth of misery to which hundreds of thousands have been reduced.

June 28th: Gerald has been sick for almost a week now, I got him transferred to a little tree in the thicket beside Eileen's grave. It is a beautiful day and the weather even at night is mild and warm. He asked for the journal to add another note but it fell out of his hand. This evening there was a glorious sunset, to the north the rolling hills of the Laurentin Mountains stand out silhouetted by the setting sun, his gaze at the little cross over the grave, several of us will visit him during the night.

June 29th: Early this morning I found Gerald's face and limbs were badly swollen, it could be a matter of hours now. Shortly after noon his Uncle Dan O'Connor arrived, how he got here I cannot imagine for it was forbidden for anyone except those giving service to come to the Island. Gerald recognized his uncle his last words as I recall 'may God bless you Uncle, what made you come to this awful place'. Late in the afternoon he died, we laid him to rest next to Eileen, tomorrow I will add his name to the cross that marks the grave. His precious little journal I will hand over to Dan O'Connor, to those who may have the privilege to read it I wish to say it was truly an honour to have known this young man.

Signed Fr. Tom O'Hara.

The Recovery of the Journal

Had it not been for Dan O'Connor's determination to get to Grosse Isle to see his nephew, Keegan's journal would likely have been lost or destroyed by the British. It was Ellen and Bridget who found their way to Uncle Dan's farm near Huntingston to give him a note from Gerald to request him to look after the girls as their father Jeremiah was very ill with madness. Dan got to the Island after a long hard struggle, he helped to bury his nephew, saw his brother got the journal and other little items and left the island for home which took him three to four days.

Epilogue

In City Hall Square, Quebec, stands a monument in bronze erected to the memory of all the people who offered their services during that fateful period of the summer of 1847 (in Grosse Isle in particular). A great debt is due to the French Canadians who took in most of the orphans, as the English speaking population was not interested but was hostile to the Irish race in general.

The emigrants who got quarantine clearance at Grosse Isle went on to Quebec, Montreal, Ottawa, Kingston, Toronto and to Detroit. Toronto was considered a step on the way to the U.S.A. which most emigrants hoped to reach from Grosse Isle. Along the St. Lawrence and the Great Lakes are to be found the final resting places of the sons and daughters of Erin with an unbroken chain of graves. There rest the fathers, mothers, sisters and brothers without a stone to mark the spot.

The survivors of the famine built up the economy of Canada and U.S.A. by slave labour on the railroads, in mines and forests. They distinguished themselves as leaders in the U.S. much more than in Canada in the political and social field.

To understand the mortality figures on Grosse Isle alone it must be understood that hundreds died while waiting on board ships for medical examination. A great many died while being transported to shore and on the beach. A large number demented by fever or horror stricken over the conditions of the fever sheds escaped to the wooded areas of the island where they died. Corpses were found all over the island. They were buried where they were found. At the height of the fever there were over a hundred deaths a day. The count of the bodies which finally began did not start till well into June 1847 when almost half of the victims were already buried.

All the facts indicate that the official count on the monument of 5,424 is grossly under-estimated. It is believed by many, including the clergy who attended the dying, that 15,000 would be a more accurate count. It must be remembered also, that the British Government and their Canadian ally censored reports about the disaster at Grosse Isle, keeping the recorded number of deaths as low as possible which fitted in with their policy here in Canada as it had done in Ireland.

It would be fitting even at this late hour that a world court – such as the European Court of Human Rights or a world tribunal be directed to investigate the alleged crimes committed against the Irish people by the British Establishment and her allies and agents. I am satisfied there is a factual case to be answered by Britain under the law of Natural Rights and Natural Justice.

If convicted on all, or any one, of the alleged crimes the said court or tribunal would have the powers to decide on the penalties imposed and the amount of compensation to be paid directly to the Irish people.

CHAPTER 9

A HISTORY OF IRELAND
FROM 1912 – 1927

This period in Irish history goes a long way to informing the reader of the British system for Ireland both north and south and one is left in no doubt that in this period Britain had no plans to withdraw fully from Ireland.

The following are abstracts from 'Curious Journey' an oral history of Ireland's unfinished devolution by Kenneth Griffiths and Timoty O'Grady, 1982.

Prior to 1916 Britain had calculated that she might be forced to give some limited freedom to part of the island as a result of mounting pressure from all over the world, especially the United States of America. She immediately set out to control permanently the part of Ireland which was most loyal, as the majority of the people there deemed themselves British subjects. They had been planted in the north-east some three hundred years ago and this area is now known as the 'six counties'. This policy became more urgent as a result of the 1916 Rising when for the first time in Irish history the Irish people united as one against the British Establishment.

In the all-Ireland General Election of 1918 the Sinn Fein Party won two-thirds of all seats and with it a mandate from all the island's people to implement the proclamation of an 'Irish Republic' of Easter 1916.

With the establishment of the first *dáil Eireann* of January 1919, most of whose elected members were in British jails, the British Government immediately set out to wreck the wishes of the Irish people. They sent over thousands of extra troops to defeat the New Republic. It soon became clear to them that with a war with Germany their control and rule over the southern part of Ireland was lost. They immediately sought a 'Truce' and 'Talks' to discuss a treaty. This was in order to buy time to finalize a secret deal with their agents Carson and Craig to copper-fasten partition and a separate 'Six County State'. This they duly did by means of what was to become known as 'Section 75 of the Ireland Act 1920'. At the same time they told the Republic leaders that all-Ireland would be up for discussion in the proposed treaty.

The President of the Irish Republic, Mr. de Valera, agreed to the treaty discussions of October 1921 and delegated the following members to negotiate – Arthur Griffiths (Chairman), Michael Collins, Robert Barton, George Gavan Duffy, Eamonn Duggan and Eriskine Childers as secretary. It soon became clear that the British delegation led by Lloyd George and Winston Churchill did not want to hear any proposals from the Irish side. The discussions would be only on what the British side would offer. This was the time for the Irish delegation to demand their say or else call off the discussions. Lloyd George, known for his skill as a negotiator, used the weak link in the Irish side – Griffiths – and with Churchill's threats of all-out total war if he didn't get his way, the Irish delegation, led by Griffiths and Collins, threw in the towel and accepted the British arrangement under the threat of war or peace.

The British Government, again, had achieved what she wanted – 'By the gun and bullet tactics'.

On 6th December 1921 the treaty was signed without *dáil Eireann*'s approval. Therefore the treaty agreement was illegal under human law. But what is more important, the discussions and the treaty were illegal under natural rights and natural justice. The Boundary Commission, as agreed in the treaty, was a ploy to get the treaty signed and approved, but it could not be implemented due to the British secret deal with Carson and Craig as stated before.

Michael Collins' position as a soldier pre-treaty was Intelligence Officer Supreme, and post-treaty Commander-in-Chief of the Free State army. As Minister for Finance in the 3rd *dáil Eireann* he was the only person who knew or should have known (as we have been repeatedly told) all that was happening in Ireland and Britain up to date. He also had seven hundred years of British rule and occupation policy to study, yet he allowed himself to believe the British again and that the treaty was only a stepping stone on the progress of unity. Bearing in mind he would have already known of the 'Six Counties' arrangement, Collins' actions, therefore, would have had a major influence on the other signatories (except Griffiths who had already accepted anything the British offered). Barton, Duffy and Childers were against signing. Collins would have also known by betraying *dáil Eireann* he and the others would be committing an act of treason and betraying his soldiers-in-arms for over five brutal years. In any other country at the time all of the delegation would have been shot on their arrival back home.

Much has been written and boasted about the way Collins was able to ride a bike all around Dublin prior to the treaty under the noses of the British, but was never arrested even though a huge reward was on his head, £10,000 is a figure often mentioned. I am not suggesting Collins was a 'Paid Agent' for the British but it must be obvious to everyone with the massive numbers of British soldiers, secret agents, police and informers in the city that every move and action by Collins and others would be monitored by the British. It is my firm belief that the British had no intention of arresting Collins, de Valera and others at this time for they needed those men at a later date to carry out their instructions and policy and to be their agents when they withdrew partially from Ireland. There was nothing new about this for the British used the same tactics at all times in the past when they deemed their colonial rule in Ireland and elsewhere to be at risk.

It would have been known to Collins at the time of the treaty negotiations that it was the best time in Irish history and they had the last chance to get unity and independence for the whole island of Ireland which the vast majority of the people on the island had supported in the General Election of 1918. With a skilled army of volunteers, well armed, in their thousands prepared to fight to the finish with their blood, why did Collins betray them knowing by so doing he would be the cause of a civil war and death to many fine Irish soldiers and many close friends of his in arms? Being by now, as suggested, an experienced soldier with the 'Brits' on the run, why did he not at least demand a time limit (say five to seven years) for Irish unity to be granted in full and call Lloyd George and Winston Churchill's bluff?

If he and others had been serious in defending the Republic at the negotiations, he would have known that it was almost impossible to expect both the I.R.A. and the people as a whole to be kept at the ready for the six months or more of the 'Truce' in the event of the discussions breaking down and the war to resume which would be on much greater scale than before.

General Tom Barry summed up the treaty, 'it wasn't a treaty at all, it was an imposition on the Irish people. There were certain facts which stood out, that Ireland was partitioned, six of our counties were to remain part of British territory and worse still, Cork and Donegal were to remain British. We still had to make an oath of allegiance to a foreign king. We had been killing British soldiers and they were killing us, because we were saying we are no longer a subject race of anyone and we had a Governor-General appointed by the 'Brits' and a constitution imposed on the people under threat of force. Redmond or anyone else could have got that for Ireland without a shot being fired and no blood spilt.'

On 7th January 1922 the treaty was passed in the Dail by 64 to 57 votes and so began the inevitable process to a civil war, the only one thing which may have avoided this tragedy was a pact agreed between Collins and de Valera in which a coalition of elected members of the Dail on both sides of the treaty would form a government of unity. This arrangement was the last chance to avoid the civil war and vital in order to be able to stand up to Craig and company to avert a blood-bath of the Nationalist population of the 'six counties'. The British, through Lloyd George and their agents in the 'Unionists', made sure no such coalition would be allowed to be formed by threats of war, with mounting pressure now on Collins by the British, for he was one of the signatories of the pact, collapsed as a result of this Collins bowing to the 'Brits' threats and instructions, for it was in the British interest to create the civil war and by doing so they would be vindicated somewhat for their previous role, as the Irish has proven not to be able to govern themselves.

The pro-treaty Establishment had great allies in the Catholic Church and they used every pulpit in the land. The Christmas Message of 1921 was 'the Treaty was a great day for Ireland'. With the treaty now passed, the task of the Dail was to proceed to disestablish the Republic and replace it with the 'Free State' under the conditions of the treaty. De Valera resigned the presidency, and a motion to re-elect him was defeated by only two votes, 60 – 58 votes. Collins nominated Griffiths to take his place but de Valera objected to the motion of a president of the Republic pledged through his adherence to the treaty to disestablish the Republic over which he presided. Both he and his members then left the Dail. Collins was appointed to the chairmanship of the Provisional Government charged with running the 'Free State', until the elections could be held to replace the republic.

The status of this provisional government which set up the machinery for the 'Free State' was of dubious legality as I stated before and would not stand the test to Natural Rights and Natural Justice.

Michael Collins' pact with James Craig of the 'six counties' meantime was never fulfilled by the Unionists as the pogroms against the Nationalists continued and, with the passing of the 'New Special Powers Act', permitted flogging and death sentences for arms offences. At times it almost seemed as if the 'B Specials' were leading mobs throughout the Nationalist areas, running wild, and murdering at will. Collins, by now, would have realized that the unity of the Island was dead and the British had deceived him once more. With pressure mounting on him again from the British for a quick election any hope of an agreement between both sides of the treaty to form a coalition government was gone and British policy of 'divide and rule' was maintained.

Collins' attention now turned to the election and with black propaganda, misinformation and censorship from his side together with the overriding influence of the Catholic bishops and with the opposition barred from giving the other side's view on the treaty, the result of the election was a foregone conclusion on 16th June 1922.

With the treaty won, the British now turned the screw further on Collins and demanded that the Provisional Government remove the Republican Executive from the Four Courts or they would take military action. Collins again bowed to his British Masters and about 4.00 am on 28th June 1922 he, as Commander-in-Chief of the Free State Army, borrowed British heavy guns and shelled the Four Courts being the main base of the Republicans since January.

On the 30th June 1922 the Republicans surrendered their main base and leaders Rory O'Connor, Liam Meadows, Ernie O'Malley and others were taken prisoner and put in jails in which may of them had been housed by the British only a year before. All Dublin posts surrendered by 6th July. Cathal Brugha came out of the Granville Hotel a revolver in each hand. He was gunned down under Free State bullets fired from

British guns.

The civil war now came to the country-side, with Liam Lynch, de Valera and later Tom Barry as the main leaders of the Republicans in the south – Waterford across to Limerick. This was a fatal error. If all Republicans in the country-side had marched on Dublin, as Tom Barry and others would have done the result of the civil war would have been quite different, even allowing for the Free Staters recruiting all ranks from former enemies, from the R.I.C. and the British army who were disbanded under the treaty.

Collins decided, against advice, and went on tour of the southern counties. This convoy was ambushed near Beal Na Mbath, Co. Cork. Emmet Dalton shouted 'drive like hell', but Collins is said to have ordered the driver to stop. He jumped out onto the road, took cover, looked up and began firing back. He moved from cover and took up position further up the road and it was there he was hit by a bullet and died shortly afterwards.

If this explanation of the death of Collins is true, then Collins was no soldier as is boasted, for any soldier, in such a manner under ambush, would have got the hell out of there as fast as possible and especially Collins as Commander-in-Chief.

On his death he was made an National Hero, a man that cannot be replaced and other great tributes that may or may not be true, I believe most of it was black propaganda to hide the embarrassment at what this man and others in the illegal government of the 'Free State' had done in the name of Ireland and who betrayed their responsibilities to the island's people.

On the death of Griffiths and Collins the 'Pro-Brits' members of the Illegal Provisional Government with W.T. Cosgrave as President, Kevin O'Higgins Minister of Home Affairs (later shot dead) and Richard Mulcahy Minister of Defence and Commander-in-Chief of the army at the same time, set themselves up to protect the interests of, and act as agents for, the British. This repressive dictatorial regime applied a 'Special Powers Act' (a copy of the one in the six counties) to suppress the Republican opposition with *dáil Eireann* being used only for the purpose of rubber stamping their actions – and with no debate, as no opposition was allowed to air their views.

With their Draconian powers now in effect on 15th October 1922, anyone found in possession of a weapon was to be shot. The parallels with the struggle against the British were complete. The Four Courts were a mock – a 'G.P.O. Easter 1916' and the Draconian measures of the Free State forces were far more brutal than the 'Brits' of Maxwell, French, McCready and others.

Erskine Childers, being one of the first on the hit-list, was arrested under the New Powers Act. As a Republican he was a Director of Propaganda, and he had been very critical of the Free State Regime, and O'Higgins in turn, disliked him. His arrest in his cousin's house (Robert Barton) on 10th November 1922 hailed the beginning of the execution of the hit-list. The revolver found on Childers was a souvenir from Michael Collins. Childers was executed by firing squad at Beggers Barracks on 24th November 1922. Four other Republicans were shot under much the same conditions a few days before.

Childers had been in poor health at the time of his summary execution and as a result Liam Lynch ordered that all Free State members who voted for the emergency 'Special Powers' were to be shot on sight.

On 7th December 1922 Sean Hales and Paddy O'Malley were shot on their way to the Dail, Hales died, O'Malley was wounded. Reprisals came swiftly from the Free State Regime. Four Republican prisoners who had been taken prisoner after the surrender of the Four Courts on 30th of June, one from each of the four Provinces, were taken out and shot at dawn on the 8th December at Mountjoy Prison, with Kevin O'Higgins being the executioner-agent for the British. They were as follows: Rory O'Connor, Liam Mellows, Joe McKelvey and Dick Barrett.

With internment without trial now in use, around 13,000 were caged up, and the regime began to wipe out the Republicans. In January 1923 alone thirty-four were executed. In County Kerry they tied nine prisoners in a circle and blew them up with a land mine. Brutal crimes were inflicted on the Republican prisoners and life to the regime had become very cheap.

The arrest of Charlie Daley, O.C. Donegal, and his death by firing squad, 'or murdered', with no redress or chance to defend himself brought the official total of executions to seventy-seven. De Valera ordered all Republican soldiers to dump arms. Many former Volunteers in the Free State army were appalled at the murders committed in their name by the regime.

De Valera formed a new party of Republican Fianna Fail in 1926, entered the Dail in 1927, and signed the Oath book. In 1932, ten years after the civil war, Fianna Fail, the I.R.A. in effect, won the general election and retained power until 1948. De Valera on being elected President of Fianna Fail and head of the government immediately released all political Republican prisoners and thus began his economic war with Britain. His government withheld the mortgage payments made by the farmers, under the Land Purchase Act, which enabled them to become owners of their own land.

It was not until 1938 that the Irish Government recovered the sea ports of Cork and Donegal. but none of those attainments brought Ireland to the land which Wolfe Tone, Pearse and others had sacrificed their lives to achieve.

In 1949 The Coalition Government declared the Free State part of Ireland as a Republic. With the six counties having the British guarantee that its having constitutional status would not be altered without its consent, partition of the Country was now final and a permanent reality to most people.

Also in 1932 the Catholic Church used the Eucharistic Congress for propaganda by its national display in Dublin. Its power was not lost on de Valera when drafting his 1937 Free State Constitution. In it was an acknowledgment of the special position of the Catholic Church in Ireland and so began the priest ridden society that is known throughout all sections of government right down to every 'Parish Pump' in the country. This exposed the true colours of de Valera and all the so-called Republicans who never intended to support a thirty-two county Ireland, as the Catholic bishops were afraid that the Protestant minority of the 'six counties' would scuttle their grand design for absolute power at the behest of the Free State Government. I will be writing on this important matter at a later stage and it will show for the first time to all of the Irish people at home and abroad the true facts of Irish history.

It was no surprise that the butcher of political Republican prisoner Kevin O'Higgins was executed by Republicans on the streets of Dublin in 1927.

A Brief Summary of the Period 1912 – 1927

This period of Irish history will be regarded as the most important time ever. The Irish people for the first time in over three hundred years were about to achieve their freedom – together with unity of their country – from the British colonial power, at a time when the British Empire ruled over half the world. This achievement was won by the blood and sacrifices of men and women, Protestant and Catholic, alike who gave up everything because they loved their country. They did this in spite of the British war machine, the Catholic bishops and the 'Pro-Brits of the Pale'. Yet the British were allowed to get off the hook by some of the so-called heroes of the War of Independence who betrayed the Republic which their forefathers had fought and died for. The result of the treaty, the civil war, and the brutal regime that took power illegally were even worse than anything the British ever did and in 1925 the final humiliation was to see the leaders of this puppet government of Cosgrave, O'Higgins, Mulcahy and Blythe rushing to London to capitulate on the Boundary Commission and agree to partition of the country. Of course they had great friends in the Catholic Church and people of the Pale whose interest are well documented,

They say history never repeats itself but, in this case, it has and one day the Irish people will see who their real enemies were, and still are for there cannot be peace in Ireland until this happens and no peace until Britain withdraws militarily, politically and economically from the island of Ireland.

It is, therefore, no surprise that both the British and the Irish Governments banned the screening of the film of the book, *Curious Journey*, the excuse, as always, that a war was in progress at the present time in the six counties and many British solders have died there. But the loss of Irish soldiers did not matter. The truth is that both governments are afraid that the general public would see that those Irish Patriots were not, as the 'Brits' would have us believe, members of murder gangs or rats or vermin. The truth, and nothing but the truth, of Britain's occupation of Ireland and of the Irish Government's cover-up of the events in this vital period of Irish history will be clarified and proven during the course of this book.

CHAPTER 10

THE AMERICAN CONNECTION

Eamonn de Valera's eighteen months' visit to America at the end of 1919 was to promote the recognition of the Irish Republic and to raise funds to maintain it. The fund raising was very successful, but he failed to get recognition for the Republic from the American Government. The following are abstracts from the Joseph McGarry papers – by Dr. Patrick McCarton whose papers are now in the National Library of Ireland.

Why did de Valera as President ignore the Republic and concentrate on 'self determination' and a year or so later in an interview refuse an offer of recognition by the Soviet Union Government? Was his refusal, as mentioned by some, because it might do harm to his efforts in Washington? This is not the case, as he had already been turned down by Washington in a country of over 25,000,000 Irish.

In April 1921 both de Valera and Michael Collins made sweeping statements to the American people (especially the Irish) quoting de Valera that Sinn Fein will not enter peace negotiations that do not provide for the recognition of the Irish Republic and completely free, politically, Ireland from England. Quoting Collins: 'We have been fighting for 750 years for freedom from England and I see no reason why we cannot go on for a long time still. We are going on until we win, because I know the strength of our forces and I know our position is infinitely stronger throughout the world. We have got them beaten today so, naturally, the worst stages are over. We are now coming to the final. Our army is becoming stronger everyday, its morale is improving and efficiency is increasing . . . The British cabinet is following a policy of deliberate terrorism to prepare Ireland for partition . . . We do not intend to have Lloyd George put a little red spot on one corner of the map of Ireland and call it part of England as he does Gibraltar.

'We are not going to campaign in Ulster against Sir James Craig, but against partition. We know that Ulster cannot live without the south of Ireland. We know that the Irish people do not want partition and we stand upon that principle.' Yet in a matter of only eight months, December 1922, he and his negotiators to the treaty, signed away the Irish Republic, signed away the six counties and plunged the country into a civil war.

Much has been said and written about the negotiators having no alternative under the threat of war or peace. Others would say, and I agree, that anyone prepared to give under such threats had no business negotiating. It is stated that de Valera's reason for not being head of the delegation to the negotiations was, as President of the Irish Republic his services would be best spent at home where he was needed. It could also be that he knew from his recent trip to London to see Lloyd George and James Craig that a Republic was out of the question at the negotiations and he was satisfied with the offer of Dominion Home Rule made by Lloyd George. Being a cute politician he kept up the pretence that he stood for the Republic and nothing else.

Why then did de Valera denounce the treaty as negotiated, and resign the Presidency of the Republic? It is said that he believed he could get the treaty voted out, and if not, he could rely on the result of the civil war to take power.

In the meantime he needed the I.R.A. and the people's support so his hard line speeches were essential at this critical time to have any chance to succeed. He had to manoeuvre in both camps and his skills as a politician out manoeuvred all his hardline opponents and friends alike.

The coalition pact signed by both Collins and de Valera on 20th May was ratified by Sinn Fein at their Ard Fheis on 23rd May 1922. Its purpose as seen by its sponsors – Harry Boland and Liam Mellows – was to take the treaty split out of the vote and to maintain unity on all sides and that the principle of the Republic could be held. But, again, Collins and Griffiths bowed to the British pressure and threats of war and broke the pact and declared war on the Republicans on 28th June 1922. (See also pages 71/72 Chapter 9.)

If Collins had been a real patriot with a first hand account of what this civil war was going to do – men like Cathal Brugha, Harry Boland and others shot dead in a matter of days – by the end of June he would have seen that the treaty could not produce peace. He had a choice between keeping the coalition pact or his pact with Britain. He chose to do the British dirty work, break with and murder his own former comrades. This is the man, both friend and foe alike, honoured 'as Ireland's hero' by all accounts, written and spoken, which we are bound to believe.

I have come to the conclusion that Collins, de Valera, the Catholic bishops and the people of the 'Pale' were all agents for the British. The record of the Irish Catholic bishops from Adrian Bull 1172, right through to the present time shows that they helped the oppressors against a people rightly struggling to be free.

With the death of Collins on 22nd August 1922, the Free State regime began, in November 1922, a ruthless policy and executed all who were a threat. The list had been argued in advance with the full consent of, and demands by, the bishops and the British.

To conclude this vital period in Irish history, it is true that the failure of the Irish Republic had nothing to do with the power and threats of the British. Nor was it to do with the war-weary people of Ireland as most authors and commentators would like us to believe by their massive misinformation, censorship and black propaganda. The facts were, that the Irish people, as a whole, for the first time since 1172, united in their demand to make Ireland Free. With the 'Brits' on the run and requesting 'a truce', the Republic of Easter 1916 was there for the taking. The people in the general election of 1918 for all-Ireland had voted by a massive majority for it and gave the Republic leaders a mandate to demand and maintain it. Why, then, was Britain so successful in her demand to keep Ireland in bondage without a shot being fired by her since the 'truce'?

The Irish Catholic bishops were the main cause of the Irish Republic's failure and it was they who were the main cause of all previous failures when Irish people struggled and died to be free. The propaganda to the Irish people had always been, and still is, that Britain was Ireland's number one enemy. The sad fact was that only a few knew the real enemy of the Irish people, and that enemy was, and still is, the Catholic bishops. They used their power and privilege to demand that Rome's rule was to apply to southern Ireland. They knew that the people of the six county state would not join a 'Popist State' so an Irish Republic was out of the question as far as the bishops were concerned. This in turn put great pressure on the weak men who were charged with the responsibility of defending the Republic. Yet again the 'Brits' agents in Ireland succeeded with their plans, for the British, as always, knew they could rely on the bishops to do their bidding in concert with their other agents in the illegal government regime of Michael Collins, William Cosgrave, Kevin O'Higgins, Richard Mulcahy, Aurther Griffiths and many junior members.

Although de Valera was officially on the Republic side, the British always knew they could rely on him (see p. 69 chapter 9) as an agent when it mattered most and future events testify this to be the case.

It is no coincidence that all those fine men who fought for Irish freedom and an Irish Republic were killed in action in the manner that the Establishment would like us to believe, (see pp. 10, 73, chapters 2 and 9), men like Pearce, Connolly, Mellows, Childers, Boland, Brugha, O'Connor, McKelvey, Barrett, Lynch and many others, together with all the fine men who were prisoners and executed without trial. In most cases the British dirty work was done for them by Irishmen.

It is my firm belief that all the above, and others, executed, were part of a hit-list drawn up by the 'Brits', the Catholic bishops and 'the Regime' for they were deemed to be a major threat to their power and grand design for Ireland. It must be remembered that during all this and previous events no bishop was shot by the Irish people. As a result they felt immune to any executions. Had there been some at this critical period, Irish history could have been very different.

It is very difficult to say to what extent the Irish in America had any effect on the fight for Irish freedom during this period. One thing is clear, they were most generous with funds without which the struggle would have been very hard and may have collapsed. Men like Joseph McGarrity, John Devoy, Judge Daniel Cohalan, Judge John Goff and Luke Dillon played a major role in the fund raising and were involved in day to day activities in connection with the Irish struggle. Joseph McGarrity arrived in Philadelphia, U.S.A. in 1890. He was born in Carrigmore, County Tyrone, and worked and corresponded with all the great Irish figures of his time such as Devoy, Hobson, Clarke, Pearce, McDermott, Casement, de Valera, Mellows, Bolland, Collins, Lynch, Stack, McBride, Ryan and

Russell.

It could be said that there was far too much written correspondence going each way across the Atlantic on an ongoing basis at official and non-official level. This was bound to create confusion on both sides and, with so many groups on each side, especially in America, major differences arose and splits in the organization were, in cases, the result. Likewise, too many leaders of the Irish side were travelling to and fro to America also raising funds and making speeches which at times were at odds with each other and caused friction and a lot of time was spent unnecessarily in solving their differences. There was also the question of the American side demanding greater involvement in the decision making, feeling that those 'who pay the piper, call the tune'. The problem with this was, that many of the American leaders of groups were getting on in years, they had spent most of their working lives in America and were retired or in the process of becoming so, they had done very well for themselves in monetary and political terms and now, with time on their hands, they focused their minds on the Old Country, dreaming that it and its people had stood still for the past fifty or sixty years.

There is no doubt they had the best of intentions but, at this time in Ireland, good intentions could lead to a disaster, and with the failure of the American Government to recognize 'The Irish Republic' it should have been clear to them that any greater say by them in the struggle would play into the hands of both the British and American agents who by now had infiltrated all groups and families of Irish origin with the result that vital information could lead to loss of life and hamper the cause.

The same applied to the Irish side. The ever increasing presence of British agents and her American ally threatened their movements and secret information and vital correspondence would be intercepted and thus cause a major blow to the success of the struggle.

For reasons as before stated I also believe it was a misjudgement to depend too much on the American effort. But when de Valera refused the help and recognition by the Soviet Union of the Irish Republic, the dependence on America became vital. De Valera gambled and lost that the American Government, under pressure from the powerful Irish lobby, would change her policy and recognize the Republic.

It is interesting to note that as late as 13th November 1927 details of the setting up of the Government of the Republic were sent to John Hearn, Westfield, Massachussets U.S.A. by mail signed by five members. This would show that both sides had learned nothing in the way of security and, more important, it highlighted the total dependence and demands of the Americans that they be the first to have a say before it was debated at home in Ireland. Likewise, it must be assumed that a copy of the Army Council's statement and letter of 20th May 1927 to both Sinn Fein and its breakaway group known as Fianna Fail were also sent to America. It would seem that nothing concrete was put forward by the American side and Fianna Fail's reply was, 'It was unanimously decided that the Army's proposals were not accepted as a basis for discussion'. In acknowledging this letter the Army Council asked: 'As you do not indicate what the objections were on any particular proposal, is the Council to take it that the entire proposals were unacceptable?' Fianna Fail's reply: 'We have to inform you that the proposals were not discussed to date'. The Sinn Feinn response depended on the pre-conditions from Fianna Fail and so there was no agreement. The Army Council decided that no useful purpose would be served in continuing to try to achieve co-ordination and ceased its efforts. The purpose of the Army Council's proposals were: full co-operation by all Republicans in the June elections to enable a majority of Republicans to be elected and form a government and thus defend the Irish Republic.

The question here is, why did de Valera refuse even to discuss the proposals as he was the President of the Fianna Fail Party at this crucial time? It would seem that he had finally distanced himself and the Party from the Republican Organization and the Army Council and yet at the same time retained the name of the 'Republican Party' to deceive the general public into believing he still stood for the Republic.

De Valera and his Party were prepared to accept defeat in the June 1927 election so as to be ready to take power at the next election knowing that the present 'Regime' would, by then, have lost any support they had in the State.

The Regime betrayed the Irish people by their failure on the treaty, their sell out on partition, Draconian legislation under the Emergency Powers Act and the state of the economy and, in October 1931, with the state now at war, the introduction of a 'Public Safety Bill' which set up a military tribunal of five members to deal with political crime and to punish it with the death penalty. The only appeal was to the Executive Council. In a matter of days the 'Regime' used its powers to make Saor Eire, I.R.A. and other organizations illegal. Those arrested were brought before the military tribunal.

There is little doubt that this latest action by the 'Regime' helped Fianna Fail win the 1932 general election with the help of the I.R.A. The election result was the beginning of the end of Cosgrave and his 'Illegal Regime' and of the Cumann Na Ngaedheal Party who, after ten brutal years of dictatorial power, had put back the clock to AD 1172 and left a legacy for future generations of Irish people to continue the struggle for as long as it takes. All for the appeasement of their British masters.

CHAPTER 11

THE COMING OF DE VALERA

In the course of this section of the book I will be referring to, *Ireland since the Famine* by J.S.L. Lyons, 1972, and comments made by other authors.

Within days of taking up office in 1932 de Valera began to dismantle some parts of the treaty. This early action was necessary to keep the I.R.A. backers with him, for his Government was fragile as he had to depend on the Labour Party to have a slim overall majority. For this purpose he used the famous document number two. This is the document he paraded in public for the first time after the treaty was signed in London on the 6th December 1922 to denounce the treaty and now, as head of the Government, he had to prove he was right ten years ago. If this was the case, why did he not instruct Griffiths and Collins to use it when number one failed? He had to buy time and it was very popular with all Republicans to see the treaty dead.

His tactics worked well. He called a snap election in January 1933 and got a healthy victory with the support of eight Labour members with an overall majority of sixteen. He had released all I.R.A. prisoners and on 18th March 1932 allowed the Military Tribunal order outlawing the I.R.A. to lapse. Within a short period recruiting and drilling started. Mr. Cosgrave and his friends decided to form a group to maintain law and order. They called themselves 'the Blueshirts' with former Commissioner of the Garda, General O'Duffy, dismissed by de Valera as its leader. O'Duffy's aims were to copy Mussolini, be a dictator and take over power in a *coup d'état*. With both groups as private armies roaming the country at will, in August 1933 the government banned a mass march by the 'Blueshirts' to Glasnevin cemetery to honour the deaths of Griffiths, Collins and O'Higgins. They brought the old Emergency Regulations of the 'Cosgrave Regime' into force again, at the same time bringing back the military tribunal and banning the 'Blueshirts' now renamed the National Guards. The actions by the government more or less started the beginning of the end of the National Guard and General O'Duffy.

With serious unrest throughout the State, many executions and much crime, the people demanded that the government take immediate action. By the end of 1933 de Valera sent for Sean Russell, a leader of the I.R.A., to demand the surrender of all their weapons. Russell replied that all arms were dumped and on de Valera's orders of 1922 retained for the use of the Republic and demanded from de Valera a declaration of the Republic within the next five years. So, no agreement could be had and it left de Valera and his government in a very tricky position at the time, even though they had the numbers in the Dail. The Labour Party were only interested in social policy and could pull out of government on those issues at any time, so he could not move against the I.R.A. Yet, even though serious incidents were growing throughout 1934, 1935 and 1936 there was no letting up in the killings all over the country.

The government decided to act and on 18th June 1936 the I.R.A. were declared an illegal force and its Chief of Staff, Maurice Twomey, was sentenced by the Military Tribunal to three years' hard labour. The splits in the I.R.A. during 1934-1935 made the government's decision to act that much easier and de Valera in particular had achieved his prize for he no longer needed the support of his former friends-in-arms. (We will see later how he used his supreme power in the state up to 1948.)

There is no doubt Mr. Duffy and company could have learned a thing or two from de Valera on how to achieve a *coup d'état* and, better still, he got a mandate from the people for it for sixteen years (see p. 74 chapter 9). At this critical time I was born into this world on 18th October 1936 with the war clouds gathering all over Europe, with the start of the Spanish Civil War and the continuing unrest in the Free State. So the wheel of fortune had come full circle and the logic of the civil war of 1922 was worked out to its own grim conclusion. The men and women who had upheld the revolution against the State now upheld the State against the men and women who still believed that the revolution was a sacred duty. Recognition of the Free State – with or without an oath – is treason to the Republic. Mary McSwiney put it simply – she condemned Griffiths, Collins, Cosgrave, O'Higgins, de Valera and Sean Lemass and any government of both north and south which is unlawful as traitors. They then had a right to attack and shoot them down! The I.R.A. may have been driven underground but so long as young men and women answered the call of their blood and their history neither de Valera nor his opponents had heard the last of the I.R.A.

The government now set out to re-write the new constitution, the main architect being de Valera having in 1934 abolished the upper house, the Senate. Sean Lemass had made his party's position clear on this matter as far back as 1928 when he stated: 'We are in favour of the abolition of the Senate but if there is to be a Senate let it be a second house under thumb, let it be a group of individuals who dare not let a squeak out of them except when we lift our fingers to give them breath to do it.' In 1937 he set out to define the external association of the Free State with the British Commonwealth and at the same time abolish the Governor-Generalship. The draft of the new constitution was debated in the Dail and on the 1st July 1937 a referendum, together with a general election, was put to the people. Both were carried, but with 69 seats Fianna Fail were more than ever depending on the Labour Party to form a government.

The following is a text of some of the important articles of the new constitution:

Article 1 declares that the 'Irish Nation' hereby affirms its sovereign right to choose its own form of government and to determine its relations with all other nations.

Article 2. 'That the Irish Nation consists of whole Island of Ireland, its islands and the territorial seas'.

Article 3. Declares that pending the reinstation of the National Territory the laws enacted by the Parliament to be established under the constitution would apply only to the twenty-six counties – to de Valera and his government politically it was most important that what they conceived in the most solemn way, it was no less important to them than when the 'State' – as distinct from the 'Nation' – was being defined sovereignty under God should again be stressed.

Article 5. 'Ireland is a sovereign independent democratic state'.

Why, then, did de Valera not state the name 'A Republic' in the new constitution? It was due to the existence of partition and he could not then, as later, identify the Republic with anything less than the thirty-two counties for which the men and women of 1916 had died. Was it not naive to leave open a loophole for the reunification of Ireland by not writing into the constitution the one word which all others did not matter?

In the new constitution, articles 41 and 44 refer to the family, education, welfare, private property and religion. As stated before, the constitution granted to the Catholic Church a special position to control and implement all social matters. It could be said that their authority on those items went far beyond what was laid down in the constitution. The reason for this can be traced back to AD 1172 and ever since their power and influence over politicians and the people as a whole have greatly increased. One has only to look at what happened to Dr. Noel Browne's (Minister for Health) 'mother and child scheme of 1951'. His bill was withdrawn by the Coalition Government at the behest of the bishops. In other words, the Church knew best the needs of the women of Ireland. The bishops' power in the State had reached the stage at which no politician who intended to stay in politics would dare stand up to them and be counted. I will be returning to this subject at a latter stage.

With the return of the ports to the State in 1938 (Donegal and Cork) after de Valera agreed that the Irish Government would never permit any part of the State to be used as a base for attack against Britain, neutrality and isolation became the policy of the government. When war broke out in 1939, and for the next six years to 1945, the Irish people of the twenty-six counties lived through what was called 'The Emergency'. All imports were hard hit by the British blockade regulations. Exports of cattle and meat products increased and many thousands of men and women went to work in Britain. Also, 50,000 people from the Free State fought on the British side for the duration of the war years.

With the shortage of all goods in the Free State, rations on all items were imposed by 1943. Private motoring almost ceased. Great hardships were the order of the day in isolation, cut off from the rest of the world, in a time when the 'State' had achieved stability and part independence. With the war at an end and the people trying to come to terms with the post-war period, the scarcities and the hardships continued. The summer of 1946 was the wettest on record, the harvest was washed away. Then came the harshest winter of the century in 1947 with blizzards of snow that lasted into early summer. The fuel supply was almost exhausted, industry and transport were brought to a standstill. The government was forced once again to impose bread rationing to add to the miseries of the long suffering population; and because of isolation, censorship and brainwashing by the Establishment, the suffering and misery of the poor continued right up to 1960. This is an appalling indictment of the Establishment and the religious leaders of the 'State' in allowing the poor to suffer on a scale resembling 1850.

De Valera held a general election in February 1948 and lost power to what became known as the Inter-Party Government led by John A. Costello of the re-named Fine Gael Party. On 7th September 1948 he announced in Ottawa, Canada, that the Free State was to be declared a Republic of Ireland and in April 1949 the Partial Republic was celebrated.

It would seem that two of the most successful members of the Inter-Party Government were James Dillon, Minister for Agriculture and TD Noel Browne Minister for Health. On the economy, the real figures for new jobs created was only 800 people each year from 1946-1951 when the wastage of emigration is taken into account. Between 1946 and 1953 industrial production increased by almost sixty per cent, but it must be remembered that the growth-rate, which seems to be impressive, had more to do with the low level at which development started. It seems the only people to gain during this period of government were the big farmers and big businesses, both being members of the two big civil war parties. When the Labour Party's programme on social policy was passed in the Dail on 11th April 1951, it caused a major crisis in the government on the issue of 'The mother and child scheme'. Dr. Browne resigned and Costello's coalition was dead, for it seemed that the Catholic bishops were the real power in the Government.

In the general election that followed in 1951 the Fianna Fail Party returned to power as a minority government with 69 seats. The State was in a mess with the balance of payments, high inflation, rising prices and so forth. With the loss of by-elections in early 1954, de Valera again went to the country in a general election of 1954 and lost power to the Fine Gael-Labour coalition with Costello again as head of government and Norton of Labour as Minister for Industry and Commerce. Dillon became Minister for Agriculture and General Mulcahy Minister for Education; Brendan Corish Minister for Social Welfare and Liam

Cosgrave (son of W.T. who was head of the illegal provisional government of 1922) was made Minister for External Affairs. Both Sean McBride and Noel Browne refused to join the government. With most of the heads of this government involved in the civil war policies of 1922, or were sons of those who had been, it became clear at an early stage that these men were bankrupt in ways and means of getting the people up off their knees and getting the economy moving. They again resorted to the old method of cutting expenditure and raising taxes. With Clann Na Poblachta and Sean McBride in particular out of government, the I.R.A. began the border war, with attacks on barracks in the six counties and England, which lasted until 1962. The Costello government in 1957 lost a vote of no confidence in handling the crisis and the coalition fell. In the general election in March 1957 Fianna Fail returned to power with an overall majority with 78 seats, Fine Gael 40 seats, Labour Party down to 13 seats and others 11 seats. De Valera now seventy-five years old was again head of the government. His first task was to defeat the I.R.A. and for this purpose he had the detention camp at the Curragh (which was used by him in the Second World War to detail Republican activists) re-opened in July 1957. The notorious offences against the State were reintroduced giving the government powers to arrest and detain without trial. A policy of brutal repression in itself was not sufficient to deal with the growing unrest and discontent throughout the State and the government were forced to act quickly to avoid serious civil unrest.

The government re-appointed T.K. Whitaker, civil servant, to draw up a programme for economic development in late 1957. By November 1948 the programme was put into operation and began to be known as 'The Expansionist Policy' which will be considered later in this book.

In 1959 de Valera stepped down and retired from active politics as leader of the country and stood as a candidate in the Presidential Election on 17th June 1959. He defeated General Sean McEoin by 538,000 votes to 417,536.

The new leader of Fianna Fail and the government was Sean Lemass, sixty years old and very close friend-in-arms of de Valera. He is the man who, it was said, was to be the driving force for the New Ireland and yet no real progress was to be seen until 1961. He retired in 1966 having won two elections for his party in 1961 and 1965. The improvement in the economy at this period did not result mainly from the Lemass policy.

The British and world economies were booming, thousands of Irish emigrants, who had emigrated in the forties and fifties, returned home and put their new found skills and experiences to work to build up the economy with their own funds. This, to me, is the main reason why the 1960 – 1970 period was so successful – for the first time in Irish history. Of course Lemass and his government will take all the credit which they do not deserve.

Jack Lynch succeeded as leader of the country on the retirement of Lemass in 1966. James Dillon resigned early and Liam Cosgrave was appointed leader of Fine Gael in 1965. Brendan Corish had replaced the ageing William Norton as leader of the Labour Party in 1961.

The general election of 1969 saw Jack Lynch and the Fianna Fail party returned to power. The Labour Party with Brendan Corish as leader had some losses of seats which brought new men like Conor Cruise O'Brien, David Thornley and Justin Keeling, all intellectuals, and members of the 'Donnybrook Montrose Set'. Great things were expected from them as experts. Corish at the Party's annual conference boasted that the 'Labour Party will be the government with an overall majority within twenty years from now'. The conditions in the State at this time were such that if the Labour Party with its new radical policy did not make massive gains then its failure would, as in the past, leave it just a poor third in the Dail – even with the return to the party of Dr. Noel Browne. I will comment further, at a later stage, on the Labour Party whose strength in the Dail of twenty-two seats in mid 1960 had slumped to eighteen in the 1969 election. Fianna Fail had seventy-five seats, Fine Gael had fifty, and the Independents one seat.

The political turmoil which exploded in the six counties in August 1969 brought home to the people of the south for the first time the type of 'Regime' in power in the north. It exposed the effects of the Nationalist people of police brutality and their co-agents in killing and bombing the minority's properties in order to uphold the 'police state' and the Protestant ascendency with the full approval of the British Establishment. Jack Lynch went on T.V. and spoke to the Nation, what was known as his famous speech, and I quote: 'We are not going to stand idly by'. His speech was interpreted by the Dublin Government, its people, the Nationalists in the north and the I.R.A. that help in arms and troops were on their way ready to cross the border to protect the minority. The responsible ministers and others were in the process of putting the cabinet discussions into force when Lynch got cold feet and aborted all action. Pressure from the 'Brits' no doubt prompted him to say the cabinet made no such arrangements. Both Michael O'Morain and Kevin Boland, ministers, resigned from the government. Charles Haughey and Ned Blaney, also ministers, were dismissed for being involved in an alleged plot with the I.R.A. to smuggle arms to the north. Haughey was tried on the charge and was acquitted. Jack Lynch when asked during the trial period about a selected matter as to the discussions of the cabinet said, and I quote: 'I had a loss of memory'.

The crisis in the north grew worse in 1971-1972. On 30th January 1972 British paratroopers shot dead thirteen civilians in Derry city on what became known as 'Bloody Sunday'. In return the people of Dublin burned down the British Embassy in Dublin, shocked at the treatment of their fellow people of the six counties. All Dublin Governments since 1922 knew what the position of the Nationalist people of the north was. By censorship, black propaganda and other methods they kept it secret from the people in the south to prevent greater problems in the twenty-six counties from getting worse and to save the government from being accused of selling out the Nationalist subjects and the 1937 constitution to appease their British masters once again.

Jack Lynch's Government's remedy for his northern subjects was to establish 'Political Courts' in the south to deal with what is known as the gun-men. It could be tempting to argue that the same 'gun-men', the I.R.A., might have been the only protection the Nationalists had and, but for them, the killing and burning by the Loyalists and others could have been a lot worse. So much for the Republic's Constitution and the Establishment who were mandated by the people to uphold it. Had the Lynch Government acted at this early point of the crisis in the north, history would show that unity of the island would have been achieved. It was the first opportunity since the betrayal of 1922 for the Dublin Government to make amends. But like all his predecessors, de Valera, Lemass and the Free State leader Cosgrave, he had one thing in common: when in power he did nothing for the unity of the island, but used all the power of the State at his disposal to deny the Irish people their natural right to fight for unity. This policy of betrayal is well founded so long as the 'Brits' and their agents are kept happy at all times.

THE ECONOMY

From 1960 to 1972 the economy seemed, on the surface, to be booming. Yet as early as 1970 the signs were there that all was not well and by 1972 the show-down was partly official. The main reason, some would say, was due to the world recession but in general it can be seen to be an Irish problem due to the failure of the economists and so-called experts, getting their sums wrong as to what happened over the past forty years. The main policy plan of the government was to use the (IDA) Irish Development Authority to attract the multi-national companies to set up manufacturing industries in the Republic, to create jobs, to train workers with new skills and play a leading role in the export drive. While the theory was right, in practice the plan adopted has been shown to be a disaster. The cost of attracting those companies, mostly American, on a Public Auction Type Basis, competing against many other countries, some far more developed than the Republic, was such that the millions of pounds of Irish taxpayers' money was poured into this project without any real safeguards. Indeed, the IDA were praised and honoured by the Establishment for the great achievement and yet emigration which had slowed down in the sixties was now at the level of the forties and fifties. I doubt if we will ever know the true cost of each job created by the multi-nationals. The IDA's own vague cost was put in the early sixties at between £14,000 and £25,000 per job. Those figures increased rapidly each year and by 1992 the Public Press suggested the cost was up to £500,000 for each new job. Worse still, those companies are given ten years tax free on their profits and are free to transfer all profits out of the Republic (which they do). Likewise, they are free to reduce the number of workers they employ at anytime and are free to close the factory and move out at short notice if the parent company in America, or elsewhere, so wishes, leaving the Irish worker and the Irish taxpayer to pick up the bill.

THE AGRICULTURE POLICY

The second principal programme for expansion was agriculture and, as with industry, millions of pounds of taxpayers' money were diverted to increase grassland farming to increase output and exports. Also, a major drive was launched to tackle the eradication of bovine tuberculosis. More attention was given to marketing with an eye on becoming a member of the E.E.C. and a wider market for exports other than the U.K. market which had a policy of low cost food stuffs to their consumers and, at the same time protecting, their farmers. This policy of protecting British farmers, together with a fifteen per cent increase in the levy on imports from the Republic in late 1964, seriously damaged the Irish programme.

It must also be said that with the vast amount of money spent on the sector employment decreased steadily and it would seem that only the big farmer and the big farmer-cum-politician benefited from the programme at the expense of the generous PAYE taxpayer.

EDUCATION POLICY

Both primary and secondary education had changed little over forty years. The Catholic bishops are the owners, managers and, in most cases, the religious teachers of the schools. Yet the government, by way of the taxpayer, pays the salaries to the teachers and at least eighty per cent of the cost of the school buildings. The appointment, and the removal, of teachers is left in the hands of the managers – the bishops. With little or no say for the parents and the people of the local community other than the responsibility for collecting funds for the upkeep of church and school, this fundraising goes on year after year with no ending and no one has any idea how or where the funds are spent. In the late fifties, most new primary schools, built only a couple of years before to replace early nineteenth century ones, were sold off by public auction or by private sale by the bishops at knock-down prices, in most cases without any approval by the parents or the local community and no account to anyone where the sale funds went. The parents were told only that the sale of the new schools was a part of the new education programme which required all one and two teacher schools, which had not the required number of pupils, to close and the pupils were to be 'bussed' free of charge to larger school centres where the facilities were more up-to-date and the standard of education would be greatly improved.

As we now know that policy failed on all fronts for the following reasons.

(1)   The local school in any rural area is at the heart of the community. When the school closed the parents' interest in the community died as they no longer had a part to play to maintain it.

(2)   The 'bussing' of pupils required that they had to be up very early each morning and late home each evening which caused a lot of problems especially in winter when the safety of the pupils is a worry.

(3)   The massive cost of this transport had to be met by the taxpayer who was already over burdened with high taxes.

(4)   It would seem that no consideration was given to the fact that in a few years the number of pupils would again reach the requirements of those new schools; nor were the parents' interests and rights protected.

(5)   Once the government and the bishops had the programme completed the 'bussing' was no longer free and the parents had to find the bus fares.

If there were any times in the State's history when its people were brainwashed and treated with utter contempt, surely this period is one of them. As a result of this new policy no great improvement in standards as yet can be confirmed. As to higher education, the system has changed very little, only the élite and the well-off can afford this education as yet. It must be remembered that the ban on all Catholics from attending Trinity College by the Catholic hierarchy was only removed in 1970 after a lot of pressure from the late Minister of Education, Donagh O'Malley.

SOCIAL WELFARE PROGRAMME

We have seen earlier how Dr. Noel Browne's action on this matter was effected, his success in solving the problem of tuberculosis by the early seventies was due, in most part, to himself and his dedicated staff. The new programme of social welfare had three main headings (1) Health, (2) Social Insurance, (3) Social Assistance. This system was necessary to get rid of the colonial laws which were still the main system in use and were associated with the Poor Law, which the people hated. Dr. Browne, as seen earlier, came up against the wrath of the bishops and had to forego many important and vital plans which were essential for the state to implement in order to bring the social services into line with the north and Britain.

It was the Fianna Fail Party who put this system into law and carried the plan out. It is most surprising how little the Labour Party was successful in this, it being their main party policy. We will see later how this was the case. Even though this programme cost a lot of money to implement it nevertheless was money well spent and went a long way to meet the needs of the time and in my opinion it was the only successful programme carried out under the Programme for Expansion of 1958.

THE LABOUR ORGANIZATION

As said (see chapter 11), the Labour movement with the Labour Party being the oldest Political Party in the State was not able to extend any great pressures of a strong labour movement on the issues of social welfare and other related matters. The movement was well placed on both sides of the border, having in the region of 200,000 union members. Its failure at the crucial period of 1922 to dictate policy and social matters was due to its failure to offer a credible alternative to the middle-class conservative regime of Cosgrave. The Labour Party were the only opposition party in the Dail (with Fianna Fail boycotted) and had little effect. When de Valera and his new Fianna Fail Party returned to the Dail in 1927 they deprived the Labour Party of its role as the 'Workers Party', for the conditions in the State at this time favoured these policies. The failure of the Labour Party to represent the people was a fatal blow to the organization and we have seen again and again in the thirties, forties, fifties and the sixties when they were in a position to dictate policy they moved more to the 'right' than their conservative coalition partners and ignored their social policies. The electorate made them pay dearly for this failure.

The Labour Party, from 1927 onwards, found they were forced to compete with Fianna Fail for the same votes and found that a lot of people who were in sympathy with their policies, but were afraid of some of the elements in the party, were not prepared to give them additional support. The Catholic Church, too, took a hand in warning the masses of Marxism elements, which had no place in Irish society, that they would damage the moral backing of the Catholic Church.

CHAPTER 12

A SUMMARY OF THE ISLAND
OF IRELAND'S HISTORY 1927-1972

There is no doubt on the political front of this period that one man alone stands out as the most controversial figure in Irish history and that man is Eamonn de Valera. Like him or hate him, he dominated Irish public life for four and a half decades and left a legacy for debate in Ireland and elsewhere for a long time to come. As a politician he had no equals and as a president he and his Fianna Fail Party dominated power for most of this period. As a Republican 1916-1922, many would say he used the organization as a means to acquire power. Others say he was at the heart of the struggle and played a major part in its outcome. It is my belief he was no Republican, as stated before, for his actions speak louder than words and his actions from 1922-1959 endorse that view.

On the economic front the State in this period was held in bondage by the 'Brits' and the mass of the Irish people lived in misery and on the bread line with no relief for many until 1960 when the global economic boom arrived. Emigration from the Republic for over thirty years was the highest since the famine years of 1845 – 1850. All governments since the foundation of the State used the youth of each generation as a safety valve to avoid a social explosion. The failure of the Establishment to generate the means of providing work for its two and a half million people at home was a terrible indictment on the politicians whose only policy was to hold on to power and wealth, take care of their own – big business and big farmers and the like – and buy votes by placing their own in selective positions in local government and elsewhere all over the State. All others who were not party or Establishment members 'need

99

not apply, the boats at Rosslare, Cork and Dublin are waiting for you', the scum and the undesirable to leave 'voluntarily' and 'don't come back, but send all the money you can to help to feather further the nests of the wealthy'. The second tier of the political system – the Catholic hierarchy working in tandem with 'number one' – endorsed this patronage system by their deafening silence and at the same time kept up the brain-washing, censorship and propaganda. They applied their grip on the masses even more strongly in 1950, this period being the highest point of their power in the State.

On 1st January 1962 Telefis Eireann, the State run body, came on air with, to quote Desmond Fennell, the nice people and the Rednecks. With most people living along the east coast they were able to pick up the British stations such as the B.B.C. and independent programmes and yet the blanket censorship laws on books, pornographic papers of all kinds, writers and others, continued in the Republic. Nothing has changed for the Irish innocents. When the historians in the future get down to the Republic of Ireland historical studies of this period both the Catholic Church and the Establishment, being as one, will be denounced as failures to the Irish people and to the Nation and they both deserve what may be coming to them. They have a lot to answer for. With the failure of all governments and their policies right up to 1958, they set out and took the easy option, namely to invite the multi-nationals into the State. They spent the taxpayers' money on them, leaving the rest to take care of themselves and clapped their hands in delights that they had done the right thing – 'in their own interest'.

The social welfare programme, as stated, is the only one area where steady progress is now being made after forty years of neglect under self-rule. When one sees the increasing numbers of people all the time requiring those services, the progress to date cannot be allowed to slip back to the bad old days of right-wing monetary policy. A watchful eye will be necessary for all concerned to see the eventual success of this important programme, costly though it is. The Country cannot afford to be without it due to serious unemployment and other social needs.

The education programme, as constituted, will have to be reformed if the masses are to acquire the real benefits. The politicians will have to grasp the nettle and take overall responsibility for the education of all the children of the State. This requires the Catholic Church to give up their monopoly on the managing, ownership and day to day running of the primary and secondary schools. Prior to the foundation of the State there was some justification for the Church to be involved in the education system due to the British occupation of the Country. However, when the State was granted a limited independence, the role of the Church, being the main body in education, should have been phased out. By so doing it would have released the people from the overwhelming influence and dependence on the Catholic Church for their everyday needs. If the Irish people want to play a vital part in the running of their local and national affairs they will have to rid themselves of the chains that bound them for hundreds of years, a system which allowed a small number of people to do their thinking for them.

The agriculture programme, as referred to before, never came close to obtaining the results it set out to achieve. When one realizes the millions of pounds provided for this programme, it is a shock to find that only the big ranch-type farmers, middle men and the politicians-cum-farmers were the beneficiaries of most of the funds. The small farmers, who were in the majority, were left to pick up the crumbs and carry on as before. The net result, employment decreased and is continuing. Very little if any added value has emerged. Overall, results are very disappointing for the amount of funds provided. Perhaps the politicians feel that as we voted to join the E.E.C. in the referendum of 10th May 1972, come January 1973 the Europeans would take care of this sector by footing the bill.

The North of Ireland from 1920 to 1968 as established by the British under the Home Rule Act and Government of Ireland Act 1920 is one of the most repressive and brutal regimes of any state in the world. Its forty-six year history is one of a continuing state of war for the sole purpose of protecting the protestant ascendancy who are only a minority of the Irish population in the island as a whole.

The events which led to the setting up of this Puppet Regime are well documented. The intentions of the British Establishment were to hold on to this geographically and strategically important part of Ireland and they had never had any intention of allowing the country to be united. By placing a ring of steel around the six counties they were able to portray to the outside world that everything was fine and well in the Province. When war broke out in 1968 the British 'Art' in mis-information and propaganda, together with censorship, was again put into action to convince the world that they were only in the North of Ireland to maintain peace between the rival religious factions of Protestant and Catholic who were at war with each other. When the Puppet Regime was abolished and direct rule from London instituted in 1972, the same propaganda continued by stating Britain had no military or economic interest in Ireland, north or south, and would not stand in the way of unity if the majority of the people of the six counties wanted it, knowing that this can never happen as long as the British Government retains the Protestant veto.

The Puppet State is financed in total, since its foundation, by the British taxpayer. Add the cost of providing at least 30,000 troops and security forces to maintain the artificial state and border and internal security, plus the one million pounds per day cost incurred by the twenty-six county state to uphold partition and the border by the Republic taxpayers. The full cost to 1972 will never be known as both the British and Irish Establishment have now united politically and military to uphold the *status quo* in the Puppet State.

As a result of this arrangement they both are guaranteeing that the cost to the taxpayer will rise to the extent that both governments will be forced to borrow the money to fund the upkeep of the artificial State and by so doing guarantee that the war in the six counties and on the border will continue until and unless the British withdraw completely and totally from both parts of the island. I will be addressing this problem again at a later stage.

I believe nothing will be achieved to bring peace for now. Until an honest and permanent settlement is reached, the killing and misery will go on as we now know it for another twenty years. We will see later in the book how this twenty years to 1992 have affected the people of the Puppet State, the Republic and British people and how the politicians on all sides have handled the conflict in one of Britains last colonial outposts.

CHAPTER 13

THE REPUBLIC OF IRELAND
1972-1992

In the following chapter I will be referring to passages in Tim Pat Coogan's book, *Ireland 1966-1987*, and to *Ireland in the 1990s* and *The State of the Nation since the Sixties* by Desmond Fennell.

THE ECONOMY

The coalition government of 1972-1977 of Fine Gael and Labour led by Liam Cosgrave soon realized that the state of the economy would have to be tackled. With the national pay agreement and the rise in agriculture prices which followed our entry into the E.E.C. plus the oil crisis which had inflation rising at the rate of twenty per cent annually in the course of two years; with borrowing and spending now out of control and inflation heading for twenty-five per cent and more by 1975, and with the government pre-occupied with law and order, things could only get worse. When Fianna Fail outlined their policy to tackle the problems by creating one thousand extra jobs in the public sector, abolish rates on houses and road tax on cars, the end of this coalition was on the cards.

Fianna Fail took power in the general election of 1977 led by Jack Lynch with an overall majority of twenty seats, the highest number ever recorded in the history of the State. This began what became known as the 'spending spree' with the result that the country is still today paying dearly for its madness. Jack Lynch was forced to retire as leader of Fianna Fail in 1979 and that man Charles Haughey took over after a bitter contest with George Colley. This Haughey-led government set out the solutions to the country's problems, but, as always, the solutions are cheap without action and there was no action.

Like before, the IDA is still hailed as the most dynamic most efficient and effective organization of its kind in the world. They continued to spend the hard earned taxpayers' money as if it grew on trees, mostly on American multi-nationals with little or no benefits by way of permanent jobs. But who gets the profits? These are repatriated to whatever country of consequence to the parent companies. It is estimated that in 1984 alone over one billion Irish pounds left the country this way. To make matters worse, this and other such funds becomes a part of the so-called 'growth in exports'. This 'black hole' is now the biggest part of the increase in the export trade at the present time.

At the time of writing, September 1992, we have the spectacle of the leader of the government, Albert Reynolds, and a high powered team of civil servants and the IDA touring the U.S.A. for two weeks to bribe more of the multi-nationals there to invest in the State. I quote from Reynolds' speech to big business there: 'Ireland is the best country in the world for making profits'. In the next few weeks we all will be hearing from ministers and their agents by the day of another American firm coming to the Republic to create hundreds of new jobs. But they will conveniently forget to tell us how much per job it is going to cost the Irish taxpayer. In other words, they have learned nothing from their first programme of 1958. Worse still, they know the policy is not working. There are 350,000 out of work (September 1992) and about fifty per cent of the total population are in receipt of social benefits of some kind each week in order to supplement the slave wages which at present are the norm in the State.

We hear a lot these days from the Establishment and their agents of the very low rate of inflation at some 2.9 per cent, the good balance of payments surplus, the record figures of the export trade, the punt very strong in the E.R.M. and a host of other goodies. Yet there is a deafening silence on the huge national debt in the order of twenty-five to thirty billion punts and no mention of the non-existence of an Irish base for native manufacturing.

One has to conclude that all governments since the founding of the State in 1922, and especially since 1958, had no intention to change direction for fear of offending their British masters. It is also most notable there is the failure of all authors and historians, and all the other so-called experts, who are wheeled out at a minute's notice by the Establishment to do their bidding in front of the cameras, have nothing critical to say about government failures on the economy. As proof of my argument, you have only to look at, in the past two weeks, the alarm raised over the high numbers of unemployed people. First you had the western Catholic bishops getting their propaganda out first, not to be caught napping as before. Then you had the politicians and it went on from there. You would think that the problem of the numbers of unemployed started only three weeks ago and the powers-that-be were shellshocked into action. But like all times in the past, we've heard it all before, there will be no action and the Establishment and their agents will continue to treat the people with contempt until the masses decide they have had enough and demand that the Irish people's interest comes first and before the multi-nationals are allowed to take the wealth out of the country tax free.

AGRICULTURE

With the Republic's entry into the E.E.C. (See pp. 93/94 chapter 11) the big rancher type farmer has continued to benefit from the massive funds flowing into the State. It now has reached the point where funds are no longer available to subsidize at this level the huge mountain of unwanted food products which has been the case since the mid-seventies. The small farmer, being eighty per cent of the total, is no better off and with new curbs on spending by the E.E.C. many of them will be forced to leave the land and join the dole queues.

On 1st January 1993 the Single Europe Act comes into force and with it a flood of Europeans who will be able to purchase land freely for the first time. This will have a profound impact on the farming community and their way of life. I can see in the near future a situation in which the landlord and the big house will dominate the lands, as it did in the past, and we all know too well what the holocaust of that period cost the Irish people.

Since 1973, and in particular since the mid-eighties, allegations of various types of frauds and wrongdoings have plagued this sector with huge amounts of money involved, yet there is little control, if any, in the Republic. What is to do about it? The government here can say it is a matter for Brussels to solve. As I write, there are many inquiries being held here into the running of the following: Greencore, Telecom, the Beef Industry to name a few, with the Beef Tribunal being the most spectacular of all and the most costly to the taxpayer. This tribunal has been going on now since October 1991, and it is likely to be well into 1993 before it is finished. At the end of the day, as with previous inquiries, no charges will be brought against anyone.

It has come to be known as 'A Solution to an Irish Problem' and everything is fine and 'it's business as usual', except the little matter of the millions of punts to be robbed from the working people to meet the outlandish cost of a selected group from within the Pale whose fees per day are the equivalent of a half year's benefit to an unemployed person on the dole. Over the last few months the Minister for Social Welfare has reduced the amount of benefits by saying the number now in receipt of benefits is so high the State cannot afford to met the costs and, as in all other cases, the poor have to suffer. We have come a long way since the 1937 constitution which states 'All of the people are to be cherished equally', but it seems some are cherished more than others.

With the failure of the industry expansion programme to create employment, agriculture is still the most important sector in the State. It would seem that it is in the interest of the Establishment to keep it this way for a large section of all the politicians and big businesses, right down to Parish Pump level, are reaping the benefits of the billions of punts pouring into the Republic each day from Europe. At the same time the gravy-train to Brussels and other countries in Europe for the Establishment's inner-club finds the perfect watering-hole for their everyday needs. They had a few sleepless nights up to yesterday (20th September 1992) as it was the French Referendum on the Maastricht Treaty for if the French were to vote no, then some of those water-holes could dry up, and with them the lavish life style of some of the most hardworking and honest members of the club.

It is, therefore, becoming crystal clear as events unfold by the hour, that the setting up of a tribunal or other such body by the government, or other agencies in the Establishment, to find out what happened in this or any other sector, is only a smoke-screen to divert the public attention for a year or two away from the embarrassment of more pressing problems at hand. This is the way that things have been done in our name in this Republic since the State was founded some seventy years ago and although the majority of the people are, one way or another, a part of the 'cancerous system' for their daily needs, it is time now that the minority voice is heard loud and clear to call a halt to this rotten system before it's too late. Otherwise, I can see in the near future a lot of unrest and the reappearance of the soup-kitchens all over the Republic (but excluding the area of the Pale of course) as occurred in the great famine of 1845-1850. Almost half of the population of 3.5 million of 1992 cannot afford to buy the basic necessities for living at the present time.

PUBLIC STATE COMPANIES

To look back over the past twenty years to find out if any progress was made by the State sponsored bodies, one has to come to the conclusion that successive governments have failed to control the operations of such bodies in the public interest. There was ample evidence in the early seventies that the large number of public bodies was not in the interest of the Irish taxpayer, and furthermore, on becoming members of the E.E.C. those huge labour intensive companies would become a burden on the State's finances. Immediate action was called to minimize the costly privatizing of the large number of bodies which had become surplus to the needs of the State. This urgent action did not register until after the 1987 general election which brought the present Fianna Fail and the Progressive Democrats coalition government to power and then only as a result of the disastrous state of the Republic's finances.

The following are examples of some of the companies:

Nitrigan Eireann: founded 1973, its total work force 1,500. It cost about 160 million in the first ten years of operations and this continued up to 1990 before it was taken over by ICI. It had debts of 180 million pounds.

C.I.E.: Its work force during the eighties was about 14,500. It had an annual taxpayer's subsidy of 120 million and yet its losses were enormous and has high debts.

107

Irish Shipping: Total losses to mid-eighties at around fifty million, the negligence of the board and the arrogance of some of the executives and the government representatives as watchdogs on behalf of the taxpayer was a major scandal. The company had to be liquidated.

Irish Steel: Received 125 million in State grants, lost eighty-four million up to 1985 and continuing heavy losses in 1992.

Air-Lingus: Work force of about 8,000, this company was the jewel in the crown of the State, we were told by the politicians and the media hype over the years, yet the group's overall loss for 1991 was eighteen million and rising. It now needs some 700 million to purchase new aircraft over the next three years. A major crisis in the company is about to break, come 1993.

E.S.B.: In a four year period to 1983 its capital expenditure amounted to 825 million on plants that were not needed, this is why the electricity bills in the Republic are twenty per cent higher than in the rest of Europe. The work force is around 12,000 and they have borrowed about 1,200 million to erect generating capacity while only half, at best, is required.

R.T.E.: A work force of about 2,000. In 1986 it showed a paper profit of three million, but when the licence fee and other items are deducted it would show a loss. This public body was set up in 1962 for the Irish people (see p.100 C. 12) and yet thirty years later it is solely the mouthpiece of the Irish, British and American Establishments. It treats the Irish people with contempt by using its monopoly powers to censor any interviews on the air-waves and screen far in excess of the broadcasting act which they ignore (see High Court decision of 31st July 1992, *O'Toole v. R.T.E.*). With no independent service in the state after thirty years it's of little wonder that the code number of R.T.E. is the Donnybrook set, for it is in the interest of both the Establishment and R.T.E. to keep this cosy club arrangement. An independent service could damage their health and open up a can of worms which have been in hibernation for the past thirty years so that the piper can call the tune.

Department of Post & Telegraphs: Total work force 20,000. Its debts run into the billions, service to the consumer is very poor and the cost twice the European charge in the seventies and early eighties. The service improved over the past ten years, but the cost is still far too high even though the body is now two private companies. Both are monopolies with no competition and are against the public interest.

The foregoing are only the top eight bodies but there are at least one hundred smaller companies operating in the State and it would be fair to say most, if not all, are losing money. How can a State of the size of the Republic and its low population of three and a half million justify the luxury of maintaining such companies in 1992? I could write a book on this subject alone but I have not the time or space to do so now.

PRIVATE COMPANIES

The biggest companies originally based in the Republic have, over the past twelve years, been forced to make foreign acquittance and are often subject to take-over by foreigners. The main reason for this is that the Irish economic base is too small for those firms to grow and the other is that high taxation in the Republic is driving the Irish firms abroad where taxation and the industrial base is much better and as a result the Irish economy is losing out on jobs and revenue. Here, again, is a further example of Government policy. On the one hand they are inviting foreign companies to the Republic on a tax-free basis, on the other hand they are running out of the State Irish companies because of the high cost of taxation. No wonder we have 350,000 people unemployed in 1992.

EDUCATION

Twenty years have passed (see pages 100/101, chapter 12,) during which there seems to have been some improvement in the standards and an increase in the number of pupils going into higher education, though the same old failed policy is still retained. The cost to parents of educating their children has increased to the stage that they are forced to borrow the money for bus fares, books, up-keep of the school and school uniforms. By 1992 it has reached the stage where, if nothing is done, any improvements made over the past twenty years will be wasted.

The Minister for Education, Seamus Brennan, has put forward proposals for a new programme for the next thirty years and it is being debated by all concerned parties at present. He hopes to have a paper setting out in detail his plans by January 1993. In the meantime, he hopes to get a general consensus from the parties, so that the new programme can be implemented within the next couple of years. The minister has now the opportunity to grasp the nettle and separate Church and State and ban all forms of censorship by stopping the revisionists from rewriting Irish history in the school textbooks. This would allow the teachers and the children to form their own views on all Ireland's history, in particular the period from 1916. All establishments, since the foundation of the State, would like the people to forget the way it was. No wonder that we have great problems when this type of thing is forced as a requirement in the schools of 1992.

He should at the same time reinstate government policy that all primary and secondary education throughout the Republic must be free of all charges to the parents and stop the double taxation burden on the people who are least able to afford it. This will mean that the present arrangement of Church-State system of financing will have to cease.

SOCIAL WELFARE SERVICES

The Social Welfare Programme of 1958 was the only successful part of the expansion programme policy carried out by the Fianna Fail Government. We have still a long way to go to bring our system to the level which is taken for granted on mainland Europe (see also p. 100 Chapter 12).

The problem in the Republic is the same as education where Church and State are partners, and like education, it is long overdue that they be separated. The main contentious issues are, contraception, abortion, divorce and emigration. We have seen for the past twenty years various pieces of legislation and referenda on those very important matters. Yet, in late 1992, we have achieved nothing but long bitter debates and a divided public who have grown weary of the problems and have decided in some form to do their own thing and to hell with church and politicians.

The following are a few examples which shocked the public in recent times. A young woman in her teens died in childbirth in County Longford. A school teacher lost her job in a Catholic convent school all because she lived with a married man in County Wexford. We had the Kerry baby affair and a tribunal investigation and the verdict came to nothing. Then, in March 1992, we had the 'X' case where the High Court refused the woman permission to travel to England to get an abortion. Lastly we have, on a continuing basis, forced emigration about which both politicians and the Catholic Church bishops don't want to know or talk. They hope the problem will solve itself or be solved by some third country without costing the Republic money. They both have little interest in the drain of the State's greatest asset, her well educated youth out of the country.

I would suggest that the solution to most of those problems is to demand that the government's job is to govern and the Church bishops have a duty to respond and the people have a natural right to decide on all moral and social issues that effect their every day lives.

The Social Welfare Benefits and entitlements in general have improved, but as I write, statements are coming from the Minister for Social Welfare, Charles McCreevey, that he has instructed his departments to cut back the service and entitlements due, he says, to the massive increase in the numbers unemployed and the extra cost involved. The minister's instructions have now been put into action at all centres around the Republic, with senior social welfare officers calling in all part-time workers, mainly the young people in work for the first time since leaving school, and told to sign off the live register (for part-time assistance benefit) or face court proceedings. Those faceless servants of the people have no regard for the natural right of the public and this was clearly demonstrated on 14th August and 23rd September 1992 when a part-time worker was refused her benefit of about £25.00 per week to supplement her low slave wage. She had to wait from 2.30 pm to 11.20 pm to get a written undertaking signed by the Mayor of Wexford, Padge Reck, that she call to Anne Street Welfare Exchange tomorrow and be paid her overdue benefit. She had been receiving this benefit for two years without any problems. If this new trend is allowed to succeed then we are on the slippery slopes back to the fifties and, as always, the Dublin Government has the perfect solution to their ongoing mismanagement – blame the victims.

CIVIL AND PUBLIC SERVANTS

It is fair to calculate from the Central Statistics Office estimates of 1986 to conclude that the total number of civil and public servants in the State in 1992 is in the order of 750,000, this figure divided into 3.5 million, being the latest estimate of the Republic population, gives a ratio of four and a half of the population to each servant. Taking the percentage and increase in real pay (inflation adjusted) from 1971-1981 shows this sector got an average of 25 per cent increase as against an average industrial worker of about ten per cent. While there may have been a lower increase for 'servants' from 1981-1992 as against the industrial worker, it is a frightening cost to the Irish taxpayer if a huge section of the population, who produce nothing of the growth in the real economy, are in the best sense of the word a burden on the State.

The question is, how much longer is this top heavy monster going to be allowed to stay on the backs of the producer? It will be determined by the general public, for the records show down through the years the Establishment and politicians have no intention to change or reduce it. It is of little wonder, therefore, that we had mass emigration all during the eighties and now in 1992 our surplus of needy people has to stay put in the Republic for both the 'Yanks' and 'Brits' have informed us, our services with them are not required at present, but we can apply again when the storm clouds pass. In the meantime, join the dole queue and see how the other half lives. Acquaint yourself with the arrogance and contempt with which the senior staff of those exchanges treat the public, which no doubt is on the Establishment's instruction to make the dole-seeker feel small and guilty for living on the back of the State. As stated before, when governments mis-manage – blame the victims.

POLITICS

I have stated 1972 was a very violent year in the north of Ireland and the Establishment in the south became very nervous of a spillover into the Republic. The Government of Fianna Fail brought in a bill on 28th November 1972 amending the Offences Against The State Act 1938. Its purpose was to change the law so it would be possible for a Chief-

Superintendent of the Garda to get a conviction by swearing in court that he believed the person accused to be a member of the I.R.A. Fines or imprisonment for one year to be imposed on persons refusing to give an account of their movements. This Bill also limited R.T.E.'s freedom to report on I.R.A. affairs. Both Conor Cruise O'Brien, now a member of the Labour Party, and Liam Cosgrave of Fine Gael, were against the Bill. O'Brien was asked but, he was not prepared to give the government a blank cheque for the takeover of R.T.E. and giving such powers to the Garda, yet a couple of years later both these men, when in government from 1973-1977, passed emergency legislation which was far more Draconian than any previous measures. On 1st December 1972 two bombs exploded in Dublin and people were killed and injured. Both Cosgrave and O'Brien went into the Dail and voted with the government. The Bill was passed by 69 votes to 22 votes early on 2nd December 1972.

We had a new government of a National Coalition of Fine Gael and the Labour Party early 1973 with Liam Cosgrave as leader and Brendan Corish as deputy-leader. This coalition of 1973-1977, as referred to here before, exposed the heavy handed methods applied to the security crisis and it became known later as 'The Heavy Gang'. The Garda, seemingly immune from prosecution, suppressed the Republicans with what might, by some, be compared to the brutality of foreign dictatorial regimes.

With most of their term of office spent dealing with law and order no attention was paid to the grave economic crisis. Then we had the Michael Gaughan and Frank Stagg affair, both died on hunger strike in British jails. We had the Sunningdale Agreement and in January 1974 we had a new law under which people accused of 'murder' in the North could be arrested and tried in the Republic. We had more bombs in Dublin and County Monaghan killing thirty people on 17th May 1974 known as 'Bloody Friday', and at the time of writing no one has been charged with any of those horrible offences. It is my belief that, those bombings might, possibly, have been the work of the 'dirty tricks' department of the British Establishment to influence and pressure the Irish Government and the liberal minded section of politicians to vote for hard measures to deal with Republicans and at the same time to influence the type and make-up of future governments of the Republic. And, if that is the case, then the assassination of the British Ambassador, Christopher

Ewart-Briggs, might well have been an act of reprisal.

We had the Presidential affair in which the president of Ireland resigned. Then came 1976 and the O'Brien (now Minister for Posts and Telegraphs) saga of putting the blinkers on the papers and R.T.E. This is the 'Liberal' who a few years earlier in 1972 had denounced similar restrictions. He barred members of the registered Sinn Fein party and others from using the people's T.V. and radio. At the same time he restricted the editors of the public press from expressing Republican policy. Note, this legislation is still in force at the time of writing, October 1992.

As a direct result of the behaviour of this government and especially that of the Ministers O'Brien and Cooney they lost the general election in 1977. Fianna Fail came back to form a new government by the largest majority in the history of the State – 'The people had spoken'. The Fianna Fail victory was the brain-child of Martin O'Donoghue's 'Borrow now pay later manifesto'. It abolished road tax on cars, housing rates and spent its way out of a crisis.

Liam Cosgrave resigned as leader of Fina Gael immediately after he lost the election and Garret Fitzgerald became leader. Within two years the economy was out of control and to everyone's surprise Jack Lynch was forced to resign in 1979 and Charles Haughey became leader of Fianna Fail and head of government when he defeated 'Lynch's Man' George Colley on the vote. It is said Jack Lynch's downfall was due to the loss of two by-elections in his own Cork city. I believe it was caused by his 'U-turn' on the Northern crisis of 1969 and his nod and wink to the British to allow them to overfly our territory, seen by many of his fellow politicians, and people in general, as the beginning of a sellout of our sovereignty which was fought and won by the blood of so many Irish people over such a long period. To sum up Jack Lynch's period in office, he was a weak leader and as such took the easy way out. When the going got rough, he was the first leader since 1922 in a position to influence the crisis in the six counties in 1969 and set a 'Marker' for Irish unity. He failed the test and like all his predecessors became another in the long list of Irish leaders, an agent for the British. Of course if the Montrose and the Donnybrook Set had their way the 'Nice Man' would still be leader of the Republic, (as they still call him).

Charles Haughey's first major statement to the Nation in January

1980 showed he had a clear grasp of the present problems on the economy and that we were living way beyond our means. A period of belt-tightening would have to be adopted at once in order to get the finances back under control, for the economy as a whole was heading for the rocks and emergency action was required now.

Haughey's assessment of the economy and his action to deal with it received the approval of the majority of the population as a result of this speech. It came as a bombshell to all to see his policies on all fronts were the opposite to the solutions of his statement. The Republic's economy and the finances got worse and the country was plunged into a political and economic crisis, which was to become a long and bigger struggle for which we are still paying today.

Haughey's answer to the crisis was to deflect the economic problems by dealing with the Anglo-Irish relations and to this end we are told he got on very well with Mrs. Thatcher, the British Prime Minister, who became leader in Britain at around the same time as Haughey. So well did both of them get on, the people here were led to believe that Irish unity was now a real prospect and that the seven hundred years of British occupation was to end.

The people's dream or 'Haughey's madness' was soon to get a rude awakening with the hunger strike in Long-Kesh in 1980, where Republican prisoners were demanding political status (as previously held). The Thatcher Government refused the right of prisoners to wear their own clothes even though agreement to this and other matters had been reached and in which Haughey played a major role.

The British action to allow all ten prisoners led by Bobby Sands to die was a bombshell and a kick in the teeth to the Irish people and to Haughey himself who had staked his political career on the unity question and good Anglo-Irish relations. There have been suggestions that, if Haughey had stood up to Thatcher over the hunger-strikers and had demanded and insisted on action by the U.N. and E.E.C., the Irish people, in their entirety, would have backed him as a national hero and leader. The 'Brits' would not have been able to disregard the ensuing international outcry. But, as with Lynch in 1969, the 'Brits' knew they could call the bluff of all Irish leaders right down the years and Haughey was no different. He bowed to their pressure and allowed a fine opportunity to be lost.

A long bitter period in both Angle-Irish relations and Irish politics began with Haughey's and Fianna Fail's credibility throughout the country swept away. They lost the June 1981 general election to Fine Gael/Labour Party coalition led by Garret Fitzgerald and Michael O'Leary as deputy. This coalition period in office lasted for only six months. They fell on the budget in January 1982 and on 9th March 1982 the Dail met and elected Fianna Fail to govern, again with Haughey as leader even though the Party was split open with the Haughey factor versus the Des O'Malley factor. This sparring continued and the country was allowed to drift and the government and politicians were pre-occupied with holding on to power and wealth.

Bill Loughnane died on 18th October 1982 and Jim Gibbons had a heart attack. As a result of a no confidence motion Fianna Fail lost the vote and were out of office again after the general election on 24th November 1982. The long knives of the O'Malley factor were out for Haughey's blood.

Fine Gael and the Labour Party formed the government in a coalition with Fitzgerald as leader and Dick Spring as deputy. Spring had replaced Michael O'Leary who had resigned as leader and a member of the Labour Party on 28th October 1982. The coalition period from 1983-1987 had begun with little or any prospect of stable government.

The Fitzgerald/Spring partnership was doomed to failure from the beginning. Labour needed capital and wanted taxation to be raised. Fine Gael refused and continued to cut public spending. Unemployment kept rising, subsidies on food were to be eliminated, with cut backs in health and education. The farming community was in uproar with proposals for a tax on land which would only have affected the big farmer. But with Fine Gael's policy representing this section, the proposals would never be implemented, and the Irish economy was allowed once again to drift downwards for another four, on top of the ten, years starting 1973. The politicians were more concerned in fighting for their lives to retain wealth and power and to hell with the general public.

Garret Fitzgerald now turned his attention northwards on his grand 'Constitutional Crusade', and with John Hume keeping the pressure up, put forward a nice grand scheme called the New Ireland Forum. Things looked good for the 'Nice Man' whose unionists policies and views he set out to implement.

By May 1983 all the so-called Republic's constitutional parties and John Hume's S.D.L.P. Party of the north came together to discuss Hume's proposal and if possible to find the best solution for the island as a whole, even if Sinn Fein was barred and the unionists boycotted the conference and the proceedings.

It must have been obvious to all that nothing useful could emerge without the latter two parties having an input, but we all know the main reason for this get-together, (1) for Fitzgerald to make a name for himself and (2) to save John Hume's party from being over taken by Sinn Fein. When the final report was published the following three options were put forward:

(1)   A united Ireland.

(2)   A federation or confederation of the two parts of Ireland.

(3)   A system of joint authority.

Haughey now in opposition stated at a news conference that the unity option was the only one Fianna Fail would accept. In November 1984 Fitzgerald travelled to London to see 'Maggie' to get her approval to any one of the options. She went on T.V. to say 'Out, Out, Out', on all three items. So ended the grand scheme of Hume and Fitzgerald for now. It was a bold attempt by both to get the form in place, for if something wasn't done soon Sinn Fein would be the only party to speak for and on behalf of the Nationalists due to the massive increase of support they had as a result of the H-Block hunger strike, and the many deaths, (See also p. 115, chapter 13).

With mounting world pressure Thatcher's regime decided to give a few crumbs to the 'nice man' Garret when they met again in Milan in June 1985 at a European conference and both agreed to further discussions and signed what became known as The Hillsborough Agreement of 15th November 1985. The hype that surrounded the official signing would give the impression that Ireland had obtained freedom and unity. Haughey rejected the agreement at a new conference and went on to say the agreement was illegal under the constitution, but when he returned to power in 1987 he had again done a 'U' turn and implemented the agreement in full. The coalition struggled on until the Christmas holidays when the Labour party decided it could no longer support the hair-shirt budget of Fine Gael and withdrew from government. In the general election on 17th February 1987 the coalition lost power and Fianna Fail with Haughey as leader were elected on the 10th March 1987 with the help of Tony Gregory. The Labour leader Dick Spring was re-elected by only four votes after three or four recounts in County Kerry and his party got only six per cent of the overall vote and yet won twelve seats in the 25th Dail.

Fitzgerald resigned after the outcome of the election and was replaced by Allan Dukes who pledged his party's support to Haughey's government to tackle the mounting national debt by reducing house grants, cuts in social welfare and the introduction of capital charges, local government charges and a freeze on public service pay.

The former Fianna Fail 'renegades' now the P.Ds. (Progressive Democrats) won fourteen seats that denied the Haughey government an overall majority.

From 1985 to the present day one man in particular is seen or heard daily on T.V. or radio and in the papers. His name is John Hume M.P. leader of the S.D.L.P. of the six counties with his invitations to Montrose and other such places to highlight the benefits and the success of the Anglo-Irish agreement. The Establishment and their co-agents in the Republic speak and write about this man as if he is the saviour of the nation. I view John Hume as nothing more than a frightened man who is depending on the London, and in particular the Dublin, Governments to keep him and his party from being eliminated from the scene of power and wealth by the Sinn Fein party. Anyone who is invited either on air, by press or by authors of books has to have the Establishment's approval and in order to get this approval you have to toe the Establishment line. The same applies to authors, members of T.V., radio and press.

If Gerry Adams, president of Sinn Fein party, was allowed the same privileges as John Hume in the national media and elsewhere, I have no doubt as to which of them would be leader of the Nationalists in the six counties. Why then are Gerry Adams and others barred from the media under section 31 of the Broadcasting Act? The answer is that both London and Dublin Establishments are afraid that the people of this island and the British island may hear the truth of what Sinn Feinn policies stand for, but whose policies are a 'poisoned chalice' to both Establishments. This undemocratic act, as referred to earlier, by the then Minister for Posts and Telegraphs, O'Brien, was not just to muzzle Republicans, but all Irish and English people who have a mind of their own and who are well able to make a judgement on such policies as they arise and from whatever party.

The John Humes of this country can rest easy in the knowledge that as long as we have the O'Briens and others in power in the Republic his praises are guaranteed. Note, as I write, I am hearing on the radio (at 1.20 pm 29th September 1992) the voice of ? you guessed, Mr. Hume at Montrose studio, Dublin, being interviewed for News at One on the current discussions between his party, the Unionists, the British and Dublin Governments. The gist of what he had to say? We heard it all before.

The Government of 1983-1987 led by Garret Fitzgerald is another example of how the political process is carried out with the far right party married to a party of the left and, as always in the past, nothing gets done, for each party to the marriage is fully pre-occupied in retaining their own programme.

As a leader of government Fitzgerald was a disaster and should never have been involved in the hardball game of politics. He should have stuck to his real line of work being a teacher where he can be admired as the nice guy without being subjected to the 'hustings' and at the same time being paid a good salary by the kind taxpayer.

The Fianna Fail Government, led by Haughey, continued the belt-tightening programme through 1987-1988 and at the same time the in-fighting between the two factors in the party continued and, with Haughey's support dropping, he called a general election for 15th June 1989, the result being that for the first time in the Fianna Fail Party's history they had to share power in the 26th Dail with their former friends now the P.D. Party. This was a bitter pill to swallow and the grass roots of the party made their position loud and clear all over the Republic in objecting to any coalition with the Progressive Democrats. And yet their objections were brushed aside and the 'poisoned chalice' accepted, for the taste of power and wealth, and all the other trappings that power brings, overrides all best intentions and principles. They can satisfy themselves and their consciences that it's only for a short period and the good of the Republic is at stake.

The total number of seats for each party in the 26th Dail was: Fianna Fail 77, Fine Gael 55, Labour 16, Progressive Democrats 6. With only six seats the P.Ds. got two senior and one junior ministerial positions in the coalition government. This was the price Fianna Fail had to pay to stay in office.

Alan Dukes resigned as leader of Fine Gael and John Bruton took over, but the fortunes of the Fine Gael party are continuing to decline to about twenty-five per cent of the vote at present and Bruton's position as leader is now at stake.

The coalition government has now been in power for three and a half years and during this period there have been many disagreements, with ministers being fired, the scandals in the Beef Export Trade, Greencore, Telecom and many more which came to a head in early 1992 when Charles Haughey was forced to resign as leader and Albert Reynolds took over as head of the government and leader of Fianna Fail.

Charles Haughey's thirty years in politics will be best remembered for the 'arms trial' of the early seventies, his ministerial posts in government for health and agriculture and his ability to survive in power when all seemed lost over such a long period. His skills and foresight as a politician enabled him to be light years ahead of his friends and foes alike and he dominated the proceedings of his Cabinet to the extent that many members, and others in the media, had likened him to a dictator. His support came from the rural masses for they believed in him as a national leader especially at election time when he turned them on by playing the 'Green Card' and 'Come and follow Charlie' for their approval. Yet it was those selfsame people that Haughey betrayed on extradition, Hillsborough Agreement, Section 31 of the Broadcasting Act, increased co-operation with the British on border security and many more betrayals, which left the people stunned in disbelief at the 'U' turns he made on the national question.

Many would say it's too early yet to assess the career of Charles Haughey in politics. I have no problem on this question and state that as a leader of government, like all his predecessors, he did betray the nation and its people to his British masters and blamed the Irish people for it, as always.

Albert Reynolds' honeymoon period as leader of government has come to an abrupt end in spite of all the efforts of Montrose, and the media as a whole, to protect him from the harsh realities of his failure as a leader on the political, economical and social matters which are creating havoc in the State at the present time. On the political front he is using the ongoing 'talks' with the British and six counties politicians to censor any public criticism on his government's policy within the State. On the economy all we hear is the same old 'Propaganda Raffle' that the foundations are solid and blames the world recession for all our domestic problems which, they say, is outside the government's control for now. But, when the world recession is over our economy will be well placed to take advantage of the upturn in business. We have heard all this 'Raffle' over the past forty years but, unlike before, the economy in the Republic is faced in 1993 with massive problems on all fronts; the financial money market, exports to Britain and fierce competition from Europe. At home, many businesses will close down with many thousands more out of work and the dole queues all over the State get longer by the week. Repossessions of homes will start due to the high increase in mortgage rates and the inability of a large number of the mortgage holders to find the extra monies to keep the roof over their heads. The ones who lose their jobs have no hope.

Even the one and only remedy all governments have had, and used, since the founding of the State will no longer apply for the foreseeable future to shorten the dole queues. Everybody knew that that remedy was 'forced emigration' which became known as the Establishment's safety valve on the unemployment question and all social ills within the State.

Poor old Charlie McCreevey, Minister for Social Welfare, who has already reduced, and in some cases abolished, entitlements to claimants will be forced to become the 'hatchet-man' of 1993 if he is still minister in the Social Welfare system to save big sums of money to help the hard pressed government, big business, big farmers and the 'People of the Pale' otherwise known as the 'east-coast Brits' who required a very high standard of living even during the great famine years of 1845-1850 (when many millions starved to death). *They* have no intention of reducing their high standards, come what may in 1993.

What if anything, are the opposition parties saying or doing about the economic mess? Well, Bruton of Fine Gael is touring the country drumming up support for his care for the unemployment crisis. He has all the answers now that they are the main opposition party, but when in government he had no remedies. The Labour Party, well, Dick Spring and company make a lot of noise about social matters and the like, but as we have seen down through seventy years, their role is, and has always been, to learn the 'Art' of waiting until either Fianna Fail or Fine Gael invite them to make up the numbers to form a government after each general election. They know that their leader will become Deputy-Leader of the government and others will get ministerial posts and be on the gravy-train to power and wealth, for a short period at least, before returning to the waiting position. In the meantime, they can brush up on the social policy programme for the next five years and be ready at all times for the call of duty – 'the Republic needs you'.

The far left and the Workers' Party (renamed the Democratic Left) make up the numbers game in the wheel of fortune merry-go-round and they get paid well for their services, but no ministerial post yet, I am afraid.

The present coalition government is coming to an end and with the announcement of an abortion referendum to be held on 25th November 1992, the end could come much sooner. The P.D.s may be in a dilemma and may be forced to abandon ship sooner than later. This referendum is the result of the Supreme Court ruling last March on the 'X Case', referred to before, and the government has dragged its feet since in making their minds up on the wording to put before the people. Des O'Malley, leader of the P.D.s, is against a referendum and wants legislation on the issue put in place, for there will be no consensus in the State either by political parties or groups and the campaign may even be more divisive than the 1983 referendum.

Historians will, some time in the future, be amazed that the Irish people, faced with the present huge political, economic and social problems, allowed the politicians to place abortion at the top of their priorities knowing that, whatever the result of the referendum, it would not end the matter and unnecessary bitterness and controversy would follow.

I feel the final test has arrived between the people versus Rome and the Catholic Establishment in the Republic. I have mentioned many times before that until the Irish people demand that their national rights are not for sale the politicians and the Catholic bishops will continue to dictate their policies to protect the *status quo* on this and all other social issues. It is long overdue for the people to demand that the politicians and the Catholic hierarchy get off the people's backs and get on with the real work of solving the mess they both have created down through the years.

All referenda on moral matters affecting the person are well known to be failures and if anything make the problem much worse. It is common practice for all governments to side with the Catholic Church and to frame all legislation in such a way it will be inevitable that the Supreme Court will be asked to adjudicate on points that may or may not be lawful under the constitution. Both Church and Government can at all times hide behind the courts who are the real legislators in the Republic on all matters and especially on moral and social issues.

No wonder the State is full of barristers, solicitors, judges and all the back-up systems throughout the country who are bleeding the public in massive salary fees and costs. It now has reached the stage, late 1992, that people can no longer afford to go to court to get their civil rights under the constitution and in civil cases where people can afford it, they have to wait four and five years for their case to be heard.

If the Establishment was really interested in seeing this scandal eliminated at once all they have to do is to frame all legislation in lay person's language with the result many people would be able to represent their own cases in court and avoid the huge fees and costs. It would also reduce the back-log of cases, now in the thousands, awaiting a court hearing and 'test cases', on the point of law only, in the Supreme Court would be greatly reduced and the State as a whole would benefit. But experience tells me no such changes will be made for the judicial system is a 'State' unto itself and why change when on a winner – 'the people love winners'. Remember it's your money the Establishment uses to deny you natural justice. So organize to protect your natural rights. Believe me, you all will need the best advice you can get as time is not on your side.

For those who have no experience of how the judicial system works, I would recommend them to take a week off (even if it has to be one week of their holidays) and attend the 'Four Courts' in Dublin. You will see what goes on there in the name of justice being served. No one can explain it, you have to be there and see for yourself and then you will realize what I am talking about. A study of the system for the week will forever stay in one's mind and the experience gained in such a short time will more than compensate for giving up part of the holiday. For anyone who cannot get the time off to go to Dublin then there are the local

District and Circuit Courts. These Courts are a sham and I would advise anyone who plans to attend to bring a hearing aid, interpreter, a soft chair and be in a sound mind and body, for the conditions in those places leave a lot to be desired. At the end of the day if you understand *some* of the language expressed, you had a very successful day indeed and one you will never forget.

The local courts also provide the huge numbers of local solicitors now practising with fees on a permanent basis. The attendance fee alone would be the second biggest income earner the solicitor received after property conveyance transactions which is the main business. Any suggestion that others could do this work a lot cheaper and in less time is immediately attacked and refuted on the grounds that high standards built up over many years by them would be at risk and the client would suffer.

I have stated earlier that I don't see any great changes in this area in the near future. The legislation may from time to time make some minor cosmetic changes. In practice it will be as it is now, until the general public raise their voices and demand action, so that part of the huge amount of funds creamed off from the property market transactions can be re-invested in the house building programme to maintain jobs which, at the time of writing, is being scaled down due to lack of finance.

CHAPTER 14

THE SIX COUNTY STATE
1972-1992

W e have already seen how this State came into being and how it was governed up to 1972. With continuing direct rule from London to this time of writing the position has not changed for the better. If anything, the war has intensified and loss of life has reached over 3,000 dead with thousands injured. The Thatcher Government in Britain throughout the eighties introduced a policy of criminalization, Ulsterization, torture and many forms of degrading the human spirit, mostly among the Republican population, in addition to the repressive and Draconian legislation which is on an ongoing basis at the time of writing. We had the H-block tragedy which I referred to (See p. 115, chapter 13), together with the daily harassment of Republicans only and the brutality of the British soldiers and their co-agents in the security forces. There were the concocted confessions to get convictions as a means of lifting Nationalists off the streets and keep them in prison for long periods without trial which is simply Internment through the back door.

With the 'Diplock Courts' still in action the chance of a fair trial is not part of their policy. It is, therefore, against this back-ground that one has to judge the past twenty years of strife in the artificial State.

It is becoming more and more cynical-sounding each day to hear the pronouncements of various Secretaries of State for the North to say that Britain has no interest, either military or economic, in the six counties. When one hears John Hume and his likes doing the bidding for their masters through the 1985 Anglo-Irish agreement, one has to ask is he preaching for peace or, as I believe, is he pre-occupied with saving

125

himself and his party from being taken over by Sinn Feinn? Perhaps Mr. Hume spends too much time in Brussels on the gravy-train and has lost touch with the realities of the position in the six counties. Or, does he think that the people of this island came down in the last shower to see and listen to his daily 'crap' with the kind permission of R.T.E., B.B.C. and others who have a vested interest in the well being of Hume and his fellow travellers?

The Unionists of the D.U.P. and the official Unionists led by Ian Paisley and James Molyneaux, plus the Alliance Party have no intention of conceding any trappings of power and wealth to the Nationalists in the 'police state'. And why should they when the British are today guaranteeing them 'the right of veto' to do or not to do anything that is not in their own interest? The best demonstration of this 'veto' is the performance of the Unionist parties in the current talks which commenced in May 1992 between all parties of the six counties (with the one exception of the Sinn Fein Party who are barred from the conference), the Government of the Republic and the British Government. All the Unionists require from this conference is for the Republic to drop articles 2 and 3 of their written constitution and if they succeed without having to concede any power and wealth in return, then the effort on their part, even if some of them had to travel to Dublin – 'the city of the poisoned chalice' – they were well rewarded.

It is not lost on the Unionists that history is on their side when it comes down to defending 'the Union' and their interest. We have seen earlier in this book, as far back as 1912, and in particular during the Anglo-Irish treaty discussions of 1922, how the Unionists leaders Carson and Craig had bluffed their way to demand a separate six county State. To me it shows very clearly and it was not, and is not, lost on the Unionists Parties of just how weak all of the southern leaders were, starting with Arthur Griffiths, Michael Collins, William Cosgrave, Eamonn de Valera, John A. Costello, Sean Lemass through Jack Lynch, Liam Cosgrave (junior), Charles Haughey, Garret Fitzgerald down to the current leader. Albert Reynolds, in his eight months' term of office, has done nothing as yet to show us he is prepared to stand up to the Unionists and the British alike and declare that our Natural Rights and the Natural Justice of our Territorial Right is not for sale at any price.

The succession of failures by all those leaders copper-fastens my belief, as I have stated earlier, that weakness is far too kind a word to express those men's motives and it's no coincidence that all of them rely on the same old story, 'there is nothing we can do'. But, as always, and today is no different, they blame the people for their betrayal of the country.

With talks about talks entering their final phase, all we hear from the Pro-Unionists and Pro-Brits in the south is to agree to the Unionists' demands to get rid of articles 2 and 3 of the Republic's constitution and all will be well within the Protestant ascendent State in the north. And yet the most urgent obstacle to peace and an overall settlement to the island's problem is article 75 of the 1920 Government of Ireland Act set up by the British. The deafening silence on this issue by the S.D.L.P. and the Republic's Government at the present discussions leave one to believe that they are not serious or they have a secret weapon up their sleeve to fire at a later stage to surprise us all – I doubt it very much.

The British are the prime movers of the present talks originally led by Peter Brooke and now by Patrick Mayhew, Secretary of State for Northern Ireland. Their endeavour at all times is to ensure that the British interests are protected, their aims to present an illusion, internationally, of doing the best they can to reconcile the troublesome Irish. In the talks process, given the way both Dublin and the S.D.L.P. have allowed London and the Unionists to dictate the agenda and the pace of the proceedings, the British cannot lose whatever happens. In the absence of any agenda to promote Irish National interests, the British have more or less a free hand to propagate their view of their role in Ireland. Mayhew will hope to cobble up some kind of arrangement that will suit his government and use their Irish agents as always to protect their interests and carry out their colonial policy in Ireland. To this end they have achieved their objective with the full support from Dublin and the S.D.L.P.

In the past twenty years the Churches in the north have failed in their duty to foster reconciliation. The Catholic Church, with Cardinal Daly as head of the Church of the whole island, has failed to match deeds with pronouncements. The policy on education and all religious and social matters baffle even the most conservative Catholic. His refusal to allow Catholic children to be educated in co-religion schools in the war-torn six counties is the cause and is at the core of the religious divide. By his actions he is guaranteeing that the Catholic versus Protestant stance will continue well into the future generations.

His political speeches (which he refutes), are many over the past years, make it quite clear that his role is part of the British Establishment and therefore anti-Nationalist. His appointment as head of the Church in Ireland came as a great boost to the British knowing that at all times they could rely on him to be their spokesman and that his words would be generously reported by the media of Dublin and London.

I believe Cardinal Daly to be anti-Christian in his views and actions. He has failed to address the main issue of his vocation, which is the well being of all the people on this island, especially the poor and the unemployed, who are in the majority. His neglect of this can be traced to his pre-occupation with the political front in carrying out Rome, London and Dublin's policy agenda.

As for the other Churches, at least some of them have had the courage to come off the fence and entered into dialogue with the Nationalists and one hopes that those talks will be ongoing so that, at the end of the day, greater understanding of each other's views and problems are aired for the first time. One wonders why the Catholic head and his bishops refuse to take part?

The political and economic problems of the police state have been directly affected by the recession in Britain over the past few years and with no relief in sight the position will get worse. The British taxpayers continue to finance the State in full and with the additional cost of security over the past twenty years one wonders how long the British taxpayers are prepared to foot the bill when they see their own standard of living nose-diving as their country is heading into a major slump.

With ever closer co-operation between London and Dublin in the political and military area over the past twenty years, it would be reasonable to state that the cost to the Republic taxpayers to finance the upkeep of the border and internal security would be in the region of three million punts per day. Add all other costs such as security for members of the Dail, big business people, institutions and the delivery each day of funds to the banking institution by the Garda and Army, one can then understand why so many people on both sides of the border are out of work and why the Irish government is cutting back on social welfare and other areas in order to balance the books. I have stated before, 'we have not seen the half of it yet' – come 1993 the cut-backs on the old reliables will be intensified.

The most surprising thing that has developed and been put forward by many authors was the achievement by the march of the peace movement in 1976. One author stated, and I quote; 'As the best thing that could have happened'. None of them mention that it was the British who funded the movement and we all know now for whom and for what purpose this organization was established. Likewise, many authors place the responsibility today on the politicians and the Churches for all present problems in Ireland, north and south, and yet again no mention of the British presence and their colonial policy as the major cause of the conflict for eight hundred years. It is a sad day that the present revisionists have to bow to the Establishment's whims in order to maintain their wealthy life styles.

CHAPTER 15

THE REPUBLIC'S EUROPEAN
CONNECTION IN THE 1990s

In the following chapter I will be referring to *Ireland in the 1990s* by Desmond Fennell and Richard Kearney.

If ever there were lessons for the Republic as members of the E.E.C. in the 1990s they can be best be illustrated by comparison with Denmark. Both are small countries and their populations are five million and 3.5 million. Yet when an economic crisis arises and how to deal with it the similarity ends. Even allowing for Denmark's more successful society, their advanced social democracy, their scale of operations is not much different from our own and there is much we can learn from them in the economic, social and political development that would help us to tackle our major problems. Like the Republic, Denmark has a number of small parties in their Parliament and the government is made up of a coalition of all parties, sometimes to the right and sometimes to the left. Denmark has general problems like us, but not like us, the Danes treat their people like adults and not like children and remedies are adopted to meet their grievances. The policy adopted by their government is to treat the general public as fully grown adults entitled to respect and share responsibility. Take, for example, (1) tax and other problems of the seventies: the government undertook to decentralize from the centre, to local authorities, a wide range of functions to encourage all the people to play a part and have an input into the decision making at all levels. This system and genuine public participation enabled the authorities to transfer up to seventy per cent of the Danish government within ten years.

Example (2). In the world economic crisis of 1982 when governments ran huge budgetary deficits, the Danes, like us, were in the same position, but unlike us, Denmark was able to correct the deficit within two years being the result of their government having the pride and confidence of its people.

Example (3). The Maastricht Treaty referendum in Denmark of June 1992 again highlighted the real democracy in that country and was able to stand the test and the people were free to discuss all the implications and make a decision in their best interest, which they did by voting No to the treaty despite powerful pressure from their big neighbour.

Like Denmark, other small north European countries such as Sweden, Norway and Finland, all of them outside the E.E.C., have had a true democracy for years and their standard of living is second to none in the world. Yet in 1992 in the Republic their achievements are never mentioned by the Establishment and the Irish people, I would say, are deliberately kept in ignorance by successive governments of their existence.

If the Republic is ever to make progress a true democratic system will have to be implemented and the present centralized government will have to be greatly divided throughout the regions in order that, in times of crisis, power and responsibility can be speedily mobilized for the good of the country. And this would be gratifying to the seventy-odd million people of Irish descent outside the Republic who wish to see all the island as a whole united and take her place among the small nations of Europe in a true democracy based on the trust of its people.

Many would say the only reason they, the Irish Government, brought its people into the E.E.C. in 1973 was (1) to increase the wealth of the big farmer, (2) to create big salary jobs for the top civil servants and politicians, (3) to hand over to Brussels the responsibilities of providing jobs and baling out the economy. Now after twenty years of being a member of the club, they can sit back and enjoy all the privileges of power and wealth without being responsible for anything to the Irish people.

CHAPTER 16

THE NORTH-SOUTH ISSUE
IN THE 1990s

We were told by the Fitzgerald coalition government after the Anglo-Irish agreement was signed in 1985 that for the first time the south had acquired a say in the affairs of the six counties and it marked the beginning of closer relations between Dublin and London and between the Irish Republic and the six county State. The propaganda brought to bear through the media of the State-run monopoly service by the Establishment would suggest that all problems, north and south and Britain, were now resolved and the war on this island was over and everyone could go back to their place of work (if they had one) and leave the rest to the enlightened come-lately politician to get on with it. But when the high praises for the agreement had died down the hard reality had to be faced. Nearly ninety per cent of the population in the six counties of Unionists and Sinn Fein were not party to this farce.

The sole reason, I believe, for this agreement was (1) to prop up John Hume's party the S.D.L.P. as Sinn Fein (as they see it) is a real threat to their support, (2) the British, ever since 1968, had taken a lot of stick and embarrassment world wide, especially in America, for their colonial system still being pursued by them in the six counties. The Dublin Government and the Nationalists in the north had been winning hands down the propaganda war, so the Thatcher regime had to make some symbolic gesture to Fitzgerald after the previous outburst which I have highlighted before. In return, Fitzgerald and his Government were obliged to keep their mouths shut in future on all political matters in public affecting the British day to day rule in the north and we all know now what happened to this famous agreement.

As I write, October 1992, they are at it again but this time the Unionists are involved in the sham, for how long is anyone's guess. My opinion is this conference will end soon in failure like all its predecessors because all those talks about talks were of the British agenda whose main function is to counter any bad publicity to their colonial rule and it is they who decide when talks start and when talks finish.

CHAPTER 17

A EUROPEAN STATE OF
COMMUNITIES IN THE 1990s

The following are references to Desmond Fennelly and Richard Kearney's books.

As a full member of the European Community for the past twenty years the nation of Ireland has not as yet played a full part in forming the Europe of the future. The reasons are (1) Our geographical location and distance from the centre of the Community. (2) Ireland's dependence on Britain which at present occupies part of the nation. (3) Ireland's successive politicians, civil servants and sectional interests such as the big farmers who, up to now, are only interested in getting what they can in funds out of Europe and as yet have not decided what Ireland can, in return, do for Europe.

In my opinion if Ireland as a small nation is to play a full part in the Europe of the future, she must have the right to do so as an independent nation, her people to feel free to discuss all matters that affect their daily lives. Ireland, for three centuries, has been colonized by her nearest neighbour, Britain, and for the past seventy years been divided by partition and armed forces.

Ever since the end of the Second World War a new order has appeared world-wide in the development of communications, finance, industry and commerce by which super states can now control small nations and limit their freedom of action without the need for military invasion or occupation. With this power some would say Ireland cannot be taken seriously. Others, and myself, would say the Irish nation has a lot to contribute by sharing what we have with other small nations of the world and especially in Europe. This can be done by working together for world disarmament. We should at the earliest date end Ireland's integration with the British military and surveillance network systems that apply to the six counties. Our politicians who represent us at home and abroad should be free to speak out and not appease the super states such as America and her junior partner Britain whose interests world-wide at this time, and their subtle methods for protecting them, do nothing to justify Ireland's foreign policy towards them. On the contrary, they are encouraging those super states to continue and expand their grip on the small nations as if those were their colonies and we have seen cases on a daily basis over the past couple of years how the world's organization of nations, the United Nations, is being used by the above mentioned super state as a cover to dictate her policy around the world.

The Irish nation must at first be allowed to unite her people into one nation and then her best interest would be served by encouraging her people to think and act as good Europeans, drop her policy of equal to all men and of being the mouthpiece for the American led foreign policy and that of her junior partner Britain.

The Dublin Government should at all times raise the unity question in Europe and demand action from our partners now that the Single Europe Act is about to come into force on 1st January 1993.

CHAPTER 18

THE IRISH REPUBLIC SOCIETY – 1990s

It is estimated that two million people over the past seventy years were forced to emigrate from the Free State now the Republic. This on top of some eight million who were forced to emigrate between the Act of Union and the foundation of the Free State. I agree with M.A.G. O'Tuathaigh about the emigrant experience. 'How can a country being deprived of its people and services be in a position to produce the wealth which is vital to create employment?' It is the exiled people whose production capacity is not being used to develop the resources that are available and has been successful in other small European countries like Ireland.

One member of the Commission for Emigration of the 1954 report states: If the historical operation of emigration has been providential (blessing), providence (care of God) may in the future have a similar vocation for the nation. In the order of values it seems more important to preserve (to uphold) and improve the quality of Irish life and thereby the purity of that message which our peoples have communicated to the world than it is to reduce the number of Irish emigrants. High emigration reduces a population excess (better living), releases social tensions which would otherwise explode, and makes possible a stability of mannerism which would otherwise be the subject of radical change.

Centuries of colonial domination of Ireland have left a cultural legacy where, even after seventy years of partial freedom, Irish society sees authority as a control. Another reason is the position of the Catholic Church which was a life-line down through the years of persecution and occupation. With Catholic emancipation, the Church availed to themselves a more powerful means of colonial domination over the hearts and minds of the Irish people than they ever had. With the priests of the Church drawn from its people and its authority coming from outside the country they used their power in collusion with the British over hundreds of years to frustrate any attempt to draw all the Irish people of various religious denominations to a national identity.

Many would be of the opinion that the Catholic Church of today has relaxed its power over the people since the sixties. Others would say, now in the nineties, we are heading back to the fifties. I am of the opinion very little has or will change over the nineties as I see that the people's attitudes are still firmly under the influence of the priest for their every day needs, and it will take years for this cycle to be broken. If the Church has its way it will never happen. The burden of this influence is that Irish people cannot see themselves free. The transfer of one colonial power to another continues the domination and they are helpless to do anything about it, only to say – 'Sure what can we do?' They can do plenty by rising up off their knees and deciding for themselves how the country is to be managed. They can demand their full freedom to make whatever decisions they feel are necessary on all moral and social issues, to make their lives more meaningful and play a full part in the future management of Ireland's affairs. They can tell the Catholic bishops and the politicians to get off their backs, 'we have carried you long enough, it's time we had a breather from the chains of darkness.' With the single Europe Act arriving on the 1st of January 1993, let the Europeans know that we have seen the light and have put the dark years behind us and are ready to join the fold as free Irish people and good Europeans.

CHAPTER 19

AN ASSESSMENT OF THE REPUBLIC AND THE SIX COUNTY STATE'S PERFORMANCE 1922-1992

Politically, the Free State, after seventy years of self-rule and a Republic for the past forty-three years, has seen little or no progress being made to improve the political climate, nor change in the British system since their withdrawal some seventy years ago. The Republic has been in a state of war since 1922 as a direct result of partition with a permanent border, a frontier, running hundreds of miles across country. This border has been policed by the Republic's State troops for seventy years at an estimated current cost to the Irish taxpayer of at least three million punts per day. At the same time the Dublin Government, through the Irish constitution of 1937 under articles 2 and 3, claims 'Sovereign, over the whole island of Ireland, its islands and territorial seas'. The Supreme Court in the action of the *McGimpsey brothers v. Ireland* in a test case in 1990 upheld that claim as, 'The heroic and unremitting struggle waged by our forefathers to retain the rightful independence of our Nation'.

It is, therefore, safe to say that all governments of the Republic since 1918 are illegal and are committing treasonable acts against all the people of this island. By their coercion laws permanently in force, they have obstructed the Irish people from pursuing their rightful and just claim for the past seventy years. No wonder that all Irish people love their nation but have no pride in its governments, its institution and judicial system, for they see the Dublin Establishment as agents to copper-fasten the British interests in Ireland.

The six county police state which came into being by law in 1920, is at the present time, 1992, occupied and ruled directly by Britain. It is

139

permanently at war, in particular for the past twenty years, with over 3,000 dead and thousands injured and with about 30,000 troops or various security forces in the State with martial law permanently in force. The brutal crimes they committed against the minority with the blessing of the Dublin Government are ample evidence of the double standards of both British and Irish Establishments.

As I write, being the 13th July 1992, with the marching season in the six counties in full swing, both the British and their Dublin agents, together with the so-called constitutional parties of the six counties (excluding Sinn Feinn) are meeting again to see if a settlement to the police state can be reached. Those so-called meetings started some eighteen months ago at the behest of the British who, it seems, need to cobble up some kind of arrangement with their agents before the end of this year, so as to give the Europeans and the world at large the impression for 1993 (Single Europe Act) that Britain has solved her last colonial outpost problem. I cannot see any worthwhile permanent settlement to the police state until Britain recognizes that all parties should be allowed to take part in the discussions. The only settlement which will end the seven hundred year war of occupation in Ireland as a whole would be for Britain (providing she is now serious) to publicly announce that she is withdrawing completely from Ireland within a time-frame of, say, six years from now, remove the 1920 Act which gives the minority population of Unionists the veto, remove the artificial border and let the Irish people settle what is called the 'Irish Question' free from outside interference.

Economically, it is admitted that the number of people working in the Republic of Ireland at present is less than was employed in 1922. Ever since the State was formed unemployment and emigration have been twin stories of the successful policy of all governments with the excuse that the State is too small to employ all its people. When one can see how successfully other small European countries have managed their economies, this argument does not stand up to the facts. It seems that government policy is to get rid of all the youngsters of each generation in order to save the Establishment the trouble of implementing the necessary policies to create the conditions in the State to generate the jobs required.

For the past thirty years the policy of all the parties in *dáil Eireann* was, and at the present time is, to attract the multi-nationals into the

State at the Irish taxpayers' expense to solve the economic problems and with it the unemployment and emigration issues. This policy is also meant to solve the social and moral problems that arise with over 350,000 people out of work and growing, and a further 750,000 in receipt of State benefit each week to avoid social unrest.

This policy has proven to be a disaster and yet it goes on. If a complete change of direction is not put in place very soon with emigration not an option now for the government, unemployment will continue and the social and moral fibre of the Republic will be at risk. It is time for a new beginning, but this time starting at the bottom and working upwards to lay a solid foundation for the State's economy. The economic position of the six counties police state is as it was. That is, it is funded in total by the British taxpayers. The unemployment is not much better and the emigration is on par with the Republic. The ongoing war since the police state was formed has hindered any improvement in investment outside Britain due to the risk factor being so great. Only when a solution to the political issue is found, and that means the scrapping of this artificial state within a state, can the economic problems be tackled.

I have come to a conclusion after hearing all the politicians in Britain and Ireland make grand pronouncements as to what is needed and what they are going to do, (but they never do anything). I am convinced because of their refusal to take remedial action on both the political and economic matters, that a secret hidden agenda was established between all three Establishments some seventy years ago with the result that the Nation's performance to date is such a disaster. The island's people who were the victims of the 'holocaust' under British rule and occupation for so long surely deserve better.

EPILOGUE

CHAPTER 1

The story has been told how Ireland came in the first place to be handed over and betrayed by Pope Adrian to King Henry II in the year 1172 without the consent of the Irish people. This approval re-affirmed by Pope Alexander III has never been withdrawn to the present day and most of the Irish population do not know it even existed, for it is in the interest of the Irish Catholic Church and the political Establishment to keep it this way.

A lot has been said and written about the Danish, Viking and Norman invasions from around the eighth to the twelfth century. We have depended on the Irish monks for most of the information as all the foreigners were non Christian and the press they received could be expected to be hostile. The arrival in Ireland of those north Europeans helped the native Irish to develop the country with their modern methods and today one can see the benefit of their work. The twelfth, thirteenth and fourteenth centuries saw how England and her allies, by deceit and bribery, began the conquest of Ireland.

CHAPTER 2, 3 & 4

In 1602 King James I began arranging additional plantation of Ireland followed by Oliver Cromwell's conquest of 1649. Then we had King James II's arrival and betrayal of the Irish in order to win back his own power in England. His defeat at Limerick in 1691 by William of Orange was a disaster for the Irish as they lost the control and management of Ireland for the next two hundred and thirty years.

As a result of Limerick, England held Ireland in a vice-grip with various legislations of Draconian measures which inflicted brutal crimes and torture against the Irish people. The Act of Union of 1880 was the final blow for Ireland for the population was left in the hands of the British and ruled directly from London. Deplorable misery and hardship now rained down on the Irish poor and yet we had men and women who were prepared to lay down their lives and fight for freedom as seen in 1798, 1842-1850 when against all the odds they demonstrated by their blood and sacrifice that whatever brutal crimes and armed force the British could muster against them, they did not yield. When Britain decided to eliminate the Irish race by starvation and forced emigration in the great famine of 1845-1850 the Irish people, what was left of them, showed the British their determination to stay Irish and not British as they demanded by force.

During all of this period the people had also to contend with the Irish Catholic bishops, being the British agents in Ireland who at all times were the people's worst enemy. It was they, more than the British occupation, that enabled the imperial power to hold Ireland in bondage for centuries. Remember Wolfe Tone and John Mitchel's account of this period.

CHAPTER 5

This chapter highlighted the atrocities committed by the British on the Irish race. Being experts in the art of misinformation and propaganda they set out to deceive the world that the Irish were non-human and they, the British, were only in Ireland to civilize and show them how to govern themselves. We hear the same propaganda about the six counties today.

CHAPTER 6 & 7

As a result of the holocaust of 1845-1850 the Irish in their millions were forced to emigrate to Canada (a British colony) but most went to America. This tragedy on top of the misery and hardship they had endured at home could never be explained fully until one read Gerald Keegan's journal (See chapter 8, Page 49 ff.).

CHAPTER 8

The story of the experience of an emigrant to Canada in 1847 gives a day by day account of Gerald Keegan's journey in a coffin-ship. He demonstrated what has already been said to be true. His journal goes on to identify the daily problems of misery, sickness and death on a four month journey that was to end in death to himself and his wife Eileen at the quarantine station hospital on Grosse Island about forty miles from Montreal. It is all the more tragic to find that Britain, Canada and the Irish Republic Governments all connived to censor the events of what took place, and it is only in the past few years that the general public in Ireland have had access to information concerning the tragedy. I am so impressed with Gerald Keegan's journal that I would recommend it as a must for all readers who have an interest in the great famine and what happened to some of the forced emigrants on their journey to British Canada.

CHAPTER 9

We have seen down through the centuries how decisions to 'Divide and Conquer' were used in every pretext for selling division among the Irish people – clan against clan, Norman against Gael and so on. We also see how the Tories used the Unionists to defeat the Liberal Government in 1886, 1893 and 1910-1914 on the Home Rule Bill for Ireland; and the number of times John Redmond was deceived by Asquith in 1914 and by Lloyd George in July 1916 and again in 1917. We see how Lloyd George used his secret arrangement with Edward Carson and again with James Craig when he signed a letter to state that partition would be permanent and at the same time guaranteed verbally to Redmond that the border would be only temporary.

The most damning deceit of all came at the treaty negotiations in London in 1921 with Lloyd George again in the chair; and how Griffiths and Collins had signed the treaty on the basis of a Boundary Commission being set up to adjudicate on a fair border. Collins, it is said, was assured that both Tyrone and Fermanagh, with the possibility of Derry city and other small parts dominated by Nationalists, would be acceded to the twenty-six counties, and if that happened the Northern State could not be viable and would join the south in unity at an early period. If this is what happened then Collins is to blame, for he was in a position to know all that was going on in the north and south and in Britain. All the modern day excuses for him cannot be washed away as being the 'Dirty Tricks' of the British.

Had Collins and Griffiths stood firm on the unity issue the British would have conceded, for it must be remembered it was Britain who requested the conference and a settlement in the first place and they did not do so from strength.

What followed is well known as the final tragedy for Ireland, and to this day we are paying a very heavy price for the failure, and the men and women of 1916-1921 would never have forgiven them.

CHAPTER 10

We see both Collins' and de Valera's speeches in America and we see the reactions of the Irish-Americans to the struggle in Ireland on whose funding the continuing of the war depended. On the political front there was little success. This was due to the generation gap on the Irish-American side and the difference in approach by members of the Irish delegations who travelled the United States on an individual basis at regular periods. This led to a lot of confusion and misunderstandings especially when de Valera refused to accept the Soviet Union's recognition of the existence of the Irish Republic when the United States had refused it recognition.

CHAPTER 11

To justify his stand on the treaty of 1922, de Valera had to be seen to be doing something to get back the Irish Republic. He started to dismantle some of the treaty when he gained power in 1932, and in order to hold on to power he had to keep the Republicans on his side for the time being. The 1937 New Constitution was forced on him as a result of his stance on the signed treaty. The territorial claim, as stated in the New Constitution, was again for the benefit of his Republicans and at no time did he or his successors defend articles 1 and 2 and other articles clearly defined in his New Constitution, even though he held power almost continuously until 1959. De Valera, together with his predecessors and successors, denied the Irish people their right to Nationhood by executions, internment without trial and with Draconian legislation and coercion which is continuing to operate in the Republic today. The de Valera Government's action in declaring the Republicans an illegal force could never be sustained, and Irish history over the past seventy years has proven it to be the case. De Valera tried to hide and deceive his own people from his actions as an agent for Britain who was his master.

It was not lost on de Valera the power that the Catholic Church had acquired in Ireland from the British. He seized the opportunity to refer to their special powers (under articles 41-44 of his New Constitution) over mind and body of the total population and to this day the nation is paying a heady price for his actions.

On the economic front at this time the de Valera Government introduced the development programme of 1958 based on foreign multi-national companies being enlisted to invest in the Republic under the free market strategy. With the State only coming out of the Stone Age this policy and strategy was bound to end in disaster and today it should be clear to all – with 350,000 people out of work. The only bright spot in the overall programme of 1958 was on social welfare issues in spite of all the objections from the Catholic Church.

CHAPTER 12

In the period 1927-1972 one man alone stands out as the most successful politician on this island and his name is Eamonn de Valera. As a politician he had no equals, and I have here before explained the reasons for this in chapter 11 which makes quite clear the position of the country at this time. The island's economy both north and south was held in bondage by the British, together with their willing allies and agents in Ireland. The Catholic hierarchy was the second tier of the political system. With no elective mandate from the people, they used their power and influence in brain-washing, censorship and deathly silence on the patronage system of 'jobs for the boys' and forced emigration for the masses and left no one in doubt as to what side of the fence they stood on.

We also see the Catholic bishops in action in education, health and other fields and it is of little wonder that we have the moral and social crisis of today. With the continuing war in the north of the island and repressive and Draconian legislation ongoing in both parts of Ireland the prospect for the economic peace and true democracy is a long way off and this is what the British policy interest in Ireland is all about, 'divide and rule'.

CHAPTER 13

We have had many changes of government and leaders over the past twenty years and with it no improvement in the economic position. We had a short period in the late sixties when the well being of the people improved. This improvement had little if anything to do with the success of government policies. It was mainly a result of growth in the world economies and a return of many emigrants who invested their funds and experience in Ireland.

The problem now facing the country is its small size with only 3.5 million of a population. We cannot afford the luxury of the numbers of paid politicians in the Dail and upper house, likewise the numbers of State bodies and companies which are a major drain on the State's finances. Many non-essential posts and bodies are set up and with it the overlapping of responsibilities. Confusion is the result as to who is in charge of what; and the public as a whole are frustrated in their efforts to get a service that they paid dearly for.

The political problems since the Anglo-Irish agreement of 1985 are such that the Republic's politicians of all parties have thrown in the towel on the unity of this island and have washed their stained hands of what is still called the Irish Question. They have allowed the British to claim the moral and high ground on their agenda of their interests when they chose to arrange talks about talks on Ireland.

If, as I believe, the Establishment has not learnt anything from the past seventy years, it is long overdue that they break out of the vicious circle if they want to be able to join the main stream of the European countries and ensure Republic's future and well being.

CHAPTER 14

I have shown that the solution to the north's crisis of this police state can never be solved as long as Britain continues to grant to the Unionists the right of veto and it does not matter who blames who for the twenty-five year war which is continuing as I write.

It suits the British Establishment to claim that the I.R.A. Republicans are the cause for the costly war. They use every means at their disposal to hammer home the message by brain-washing, censorship, black propaganda and misinformation through the wide media which makes it impossible for them to have serious dialogue with the Nationalists and to understand their problems. Experience tells the Nationalists they cannot trust the British – as the Nationalists of the south found out to their cost some seventy-five years ago. The British motive from time to time in arranging talks about talks on the future of the six counties police state is at best a public relations exercise to show the world her good intentions and good faith as a power broker between the Unionists and the Nationalists of the six counties and the Dublin Government of the south. And yet Britain has to accept the political embarrassment that the Northern State is colonized by armed forces, occupation, and direct rule by force by Britain.

How can Britain square this position with her black propaganda as the honest broker which leaves her views and comments on other countries problems and rights a sham? For she is in no position to lecture any country without first putting her own house in order.

Another major problem in the six counties is the Protestant versus Catholic religious stance. Here I put a major share of the blame on the present Catholic Cardinal Daly who has refused to allow the Catholic children to be educated in the co-religious schools. His motives and actions will ensure that the bigots on both sides in the police state will reign supreme well into the future – to the delight of the British Establishment.

As long as the Americans keep Britain as their junior partner and use her, as they have done since the end of World War One, as their mouthpiece for their interest in Europe there will be no pressure put by the American Establishment on Britain to settle the Irish Question. This we have seen from past experience and it doesn't matter that there are up to seventy million Irish-Americans living in the United States. With no improvement in the economic position for the past twenty years, and with their paymaster almost bankrupt and no movement to break out of the straight-jacket at the present time, the future for the artificial State is grim.

CHAPTER 15

In the past, and at the present time, the foreign policy of the Dublin Establishment is to ally themselves in total with the Americans and British in the political and economic management of the Republic affairs. We see, at the present time, that both America and Britain are on the point of bankruptcy and their only interest now is to keep a war going in order that they can grab some other countries' hard earned interest and wealth under the pretext and cover of the United Nations. This organization over the past few years has been hijacked and controlled by America and her junior partner and is ongoing today and we have seen how their deceit and arrogance is carried out. Why, then, do the Dublin Establishment continue to be part of this arrangement knowing, as they do, that the Republic's best interest is served in Europe (as members of the E.E.C. for the past twenty years) for the well being of this country's future? Denmark is a model which the Republic should follow and not, as at present, use the E.E.C. only as a begging bowl when the cash at home has run out.

CHAPTER 16

We all by now have had ample time to study the effects on the island of the Anglo-Irish agreement of 1985. One would be excused for believing that all the problems in Ireland and with Britain are solved. On the contrary, the position is far more serious now for the population as a whole for there is no democracy or public debate on any of the issues. All we hear now from the Dublin ministers and others of the Establishment is that their talks and discussions with other parties to the agreement are going well and they are making good progress. But we never hear on what that progress is made, for all talks since 1985 have been in secret.

There have been serious territorial incursions by the British army into the Republic on a regular basis, with the blowing up and closing of vital cross border roads. There have been other infringements on the rights of the people to travel throughout this island free from harassment and intimidation and loss of life. And what do we hear from the relevant ministers? They 'take the matter seriously' and that is the end of it. In other words the public have no right to demand explanations of what is being done to stop those acts. Prior to 1985 at least the Dublin politicians and the Nationalists of the artificial State were allowed and were free to voice their protest publicly and the people's views were discussed somewhat. Now it's the case of everyone having to keep their mouths shut and allow the British and their agents to do all the talking on the public's behalf. The population of this island is being led up a blind alley by the British and Dublin Establishments and they now, by their arrogant demands, want the people to trust them to do what is right on their behalf in secret, continuing seventy-five years of betrayal and mismanagement.

CHAPTER 17

The Irish nation for the first time in hundreds of years now has an opportunity to break out of the chains that have robbed her of true nationhood. But first the country has to win freedom and unity from the British presence. As a nation I believe we can play an important role as a small country and use our many talents to the betterment of the Europe of the future. In the past we have allowed ourselves to be pre-occupied with our connection with the United States of America and her agent Britain and neglected to take our rightful place which is at the centre of European affairs. The time has come when Ireland has to make a clear decision as to which side her best interests will be served by in the future and get off the fence now and not be caught with a foot in each camp as has happened to Britain.

CHAPTER 18

It is now seventy years since the founding of the State and the time has come for the Dublin Establishment to open its files and inform the public of the true events of 1918-1927 and the real terms which affected both Britain and the Free State as a result of the treaty of 1922. I am convinced, due to lack of any concrete statement or document by the Establishment, and by the pro-establishment line taken by most authors and historians, that a secret hidden agenda was agreed and this agenda is still in place at the time of writing. If the Dublin Establishment want the co-operation of its people to deal with the serious task that is befalling the State, it first must give confidence and pride back to the whole population by opening the dark-rooms of the past and begin to create a true democracy in which all Irish people in the State can willingly play their part. Democracy in name only is all we have had since 1922 and is no longer acceptable. The Catholic Church which forms a major part of the Establishment will have to re-think their position and responsibilities. No longer can they treat the people of this island as if nothing has happened to their dictatorial policy. They must let the people feel free to decide on their own moral and social needs.

CHAPTER 19

If the Dublin Establishment believes that the 1922 settlement was legal and honourable and what has taken place in Ireland to date is a success, then the future of the nation is grim. The continuing war in Ireland is costing the overburdened Irish taxpayer millions of punts a day, money that the country cannot afford and yet the Establishment does not concern itself with the drain on resources to uphold an artificial border in the country.

The pro-British elements on the island would say that if Britain withdrew from the north a blood-bath would take place. My view is we have had a blood-bath in Ireland for the past four hundred years and nobody cried halt to stop the blood-letting by the British and their co-agents and their argument against unity and withdrawal is entirely based on privileges they have received at the expense of the majority of the population. The economic problems facing the Republic are grave with unemployment at 350,000 and rising, and no government policy to stop the increase. This has haunted the State for seventy years and the nation for more than two hundred years. The people have lost all confidence in the politicians who make grand pronouncements on the subject every now and then – but never do anything about it.

As for the six counties police state, no economical improvement can be envisaged until the unity of the island is first achieved. In the meantime, the British and Irish taxpayer will continue to foot the bill.

IRISH CULTURE AND THE LOSS GENERATIONS

The holocaust as a result of the great famine of the eighteen forties, in particular 1847, has been described as a watershed in Irish political, economic and social history. It regulated the population to an acceptable level and provided the British Government, landlords and the Catholic bishops with greater powers at will over the people. In addition, with the loss of the youth of each generation since 1840 by forced emigration, the famine has caused a major cultural gap in Irish society, the effects of which are most relevant today and will be so for a long time to come – even if emigration is halted tomorrow.

Finally, I propose and recommend to all Irish people at home and abroad who believe, as I do, that a great wrong had been committed against the Irish race and nation for over three hundred years by Britain and her agents. We Irish owe it to ourselves, we have a duty to have the great wrong put right for all those millions of Irish dead who suffered at the hands of the oppressor for so many years (see chapter 8, page 64). This is a proposal that a relevant body should conduct an inquiry into, and adjudicate on, the alleged crimes which, briefly, are as follows:

(1)   Illegal confiscation of people's property and livelihood by armed force and treachery.

(2)   The denial of the people's political, economic, cultural, religious and social basic rights as a nation to have the freedom to govern themselves in whatever manner they deem fit and necessary.

(3)   The suffering brought about by torture, imprisonment without trial and brutal crimes committed against the person and their property with no right of redress.

(4)   A planned policy to eliminate the Irish race in Ireland to an acceptable level by means of coercion and Draconian legislation which enable the corrupt judiciary and the British Establishment to make judgement on the people.

(5)   The denial by the oppressor to allow the Irish majority to eat their own grown products which led to death by starvation, famine, disease, unemployment and forced emigration and death to millions of the Irish poor in the most horrendous manner known to mankind.

The foregoing items from one to five inclusive are only a broad outline of the alleged crimes. If any person or group of people who may have any relevant information or documented evidence, especially of the great famine period, and who want to get involved putting the record straight for the first time in Irish History, by bringing Britain, her allies and agents before a world court to answer the alleged charges made against them.

By so doing the living Irish everywhere can feel proud in honouring the sacrifices made by the millions of Irish dead for over three hundred years and at the same time awaken the great Irish spirit of the past which has lain dormant for too long.

I would welcome any help and suggestions by anyone as to how this momentous task can be implemented in order to prevent this holocaust being ever again repeated – 'nothing is impossible'.

My address is with the publisher.

PERIOD NOVEMBER 1918 – AUGUST 22ND 1922

A list of vital questions and answers, based on Michael O'Cuinneagain's book, *On the Arm of Time 1916-1922*.

1.   *Question.* Prior to the general election of 14th December 1918 why did Michael Collins accept James McMahon's (Under-Secretary in Dublin Castle 1918-1922) plan that he was acting for Cardinal Logue as his secretary, the result being Collins' recognition of partition?

   Answer. It would seem that Collins agreed to the plan in relation to a number of Northern Constitutions without checking out the source of the phone call and worse still he failed to demand confirmation from Cardinal Logue.

2.   *Question.* Why has Cathal Brugha, first Minister of Defence in the first Dail of January 1921, been denounced by almost all writers – 'Pro-Treaty', as a disaster, and of being jealous of Collins?

   Answer. Brugha only opposed Collins because of his knowledge of Collins' regular visits with Establishment figures in Furry Park, Raheny and elsewhere. On December 1918 Moya Llewelyn Davis had hosted a party for Collins and Sean T. O'Kelly where Collins met Barrie and Charters both British intelligence officers. Furry Park had become a home from home for Collins for two years prior to Collins assassination. It was at this address that two of Collins' female aides were arrested in March 1921.

3.   *Question.* Why, on the 24th December 1920, did the Police Gazette *Hue and Cry* publish, among others, a photograph of Collins, casting a doubt on the details described by Tim Pat Coogan in his biography of

Collins on the same day at the Gresham Hotel, Dublin, where Collins had invited Charles Heligan a British agent officer in Dublin Castle who opted out of the meal at a very convenient period?

Answer. Coogan gives details of the scene in the Gresham. Present with Collins were Rory O'Connor, Gearoid O'Sullivan, Tobin and Cullen, the 'Castle' had a 'turkey shot for Christmas'. The hotel was raided by the auxiliaries. Collins was searched, a bottle of whiskey and a notebook were found on him. In the book the word 'rifles' was mentioned. Collins told the auxiliary, 'refills' and requested to go to the lavatory. He went under escort. Tobin became worried at Collins' long delay in returning and went to investigate. He found Collins under a bright light and an officer comparing him with a photograph held in his hand. It's my belief that Collins had a 'Password' for none of them were arrested. There was opposition to Collins having constant communications with Alfred Cope, British agent to Lloyd George, and being in the company of many other British agents, not to mention all the women in his life and his drinking bust-ups.

4.   *Question.* On 5th December 1922 Arthur Griffiths agreed he would sign the treaty. Collins refused and the delegation returned to Hans place. No sooner had they arrived than both Lady Hazel Lavery and Lady Moya Llewelyn Davis called. Hazel Lavery had a few words with Collins and both ladies and Collins left together. Why did Collins, one hour later, agree to sign the treaty? What, in one hour, made him change his mind?

Answer. It is possible that it might have been blackmail by the Laverys. They could have threatened to accuse Collins of being the father of Moya Llewelyn Davis' son Richard if Collins did not sign the treaty. And, if that were the case, what was in it for Lady Hazel Lavery? Perhaps the job of Governor-General of the new Free State as a gift from Lloyd George. Erskine Childers T.D. is said to have had no doubts that Collins was being blackmailed – and for what reason.

5.   *Question.* When was Richard Llewelyn Davis born?

Answer. December 1912 and died in an accident around 1970s He was nine years old at the time of the treaty. Had Hazel Lavery exposed Collins' child he would have been disgraced. This is what he could have meant by 'under duress' which forced Collins to betray Ireland and the direct cause of the Civil War.

6.   *Question.* As Director of Intelligence and a master dealing with British agents and so forth, how was it possible for Collins to have a nest of British agents in his camp advising him on all matters but most importantly on the treaty, especially the British agent Jim Healy who later was to become first Governor-General of the Free State?

Answer. Blackmail perhaps, even John Devoy in the United States accused Healy of being a British agent and many others at the time also knew. It must be remembered that the British Establishment as far back as 1912 knew of Collins' affair with Moya Llewelyn Davis and others, and the result of this affair they could use at their own time against Collins and others and the time had now arrived.

7.   *Question.* Why did Michael Collins break the election pact with de Valera for the June 1922 election?

Answer. Blackmail perhaps, by Churchill, George and Craig, for the British feared Irish unity, for both Collins and de Valera were close friends at all times.

8.   *Question.* Why did Collins borrow British guns to blast the Republican executive, being his close friends-in-arms, out of the Four Courts?

Answer. Blackmail perhaps, by Churchill and company. Britain seemingly needed a civil war in the south of Ireland to keep the Irish people divided and weak, so that the puppet regime already established in the six counties by Britain would be allowed time to function and to rule by one dictatorial party for the benefit of the British Establishment.

9.   *Question.* Who shot Michael Collins, near Beaknablath, Co. Cork, and for what reason, on Sunday 22nd August 1922?

Answer. There are those who have felt that Emmet Dalton, long regarded as a British agent, executed Collins. Dalton had been A.D.C. to Sir Henry Wilson who had been shot dead on the instruction, some have suspected, of Collins. I also believe that Kevin O'Higgins was a British agent and the élite members of the government and army together with senior figures of the Catholic hierarchy were involved. All were well aware of the Collins affair. The following is the reason for Collins' death. He had done all that the British wanted him to do. He was no longer a member of the Free State Government since 12th July 1922. This had been kept secret by the government for over fifty years. It would be safe to say that major differences of opinion arose which caused the split and Collins found himself isolated and a desperate man. The Free State Establishment were now more or less in the same position as Britain. But, unlike Britain, Dublin's embarrassment if the Collins affair went public on the Richard Llewelyn Davis matter, the result would have been too serious to contemplate what might happen.

10.   *Question* (1) Why the cover-up by the publicity department of the govenment under the control of Desmond Fitzgerald a cabinet minister and the false propaganda published as to the murder of Collins and to who carried it out?

(2) Why was there no inquest on Collins?

(3) Why did the Cosgrave government destroy all papers and documents about the death of Collins before they were thrown out of office in 1932 if, as they said, they had nothing to fear or hide?

(4) Like Britain, did the Dublin regime fear the born again Republicans Collins having thrown off the yoke of blackmail was preparing to join his former comrades in arms (what was left of them) to carry on the struggle for Irish unity?

Answer (1) It was essential for the Dublin regime to hide from the Irish people and the world at large the truth about the treaty and the death of Collins. With the Civil War almost won the blame for Collins' death could easily be attributed as the work of the 'Republican Rebels'.

(2) If an inquest had to be held the game would have been up for the 'Regime'. 'Dead men tell no lies'. Such a man was Sean Hales T.D. who continued to demand an inquest and was shot dead on his way to the Dail where he was to raise the matter. Of course the Republicans were again blamed for the murder, but we suspect something different – the Dublin Regime used the British again to do their dirty work in this case.

(3) This regime who grabbed power for ten years might be thought to have had many skeletons in the cupboards and on file and, if exposed, a can of worms could have plagued the country – hence the burning.

(4) With the war almost won, Collins out of the Government might have been seen as a liability to the 'Regime' who would have feared that the 'Great Man' had become born again minus the 'Duress'. The little matter of suspected blackmail would then have scuttled their grand design for the Free State at the behest of the British. This, in turn, could have led to questions about the murderers of the Irish people.

11.   *Question.* Why then, is it still necessary for the Dublin Government to continue the propaganda about the life and death of Michael Collins up to the time of writing?

Answer. Collins was set-up as a figure head, hero and brilliant soldier by the Free State Regime and their British masters. He was used to belittle de Valera's role in Irish political life (see joint production of Radio Telefis Eireann and Channel 4's programme in 1991 dealing with the Treaty negotiations which showed clearly RTE pro-establishment line against de Valera). Also, most writers who are pro-Treaty have conveniently overlooked research which is available to make a balanced view on the subject. Take the biography of Michael Collins by Tim Pat Coogan – 1990 and one can see that this research was not used to complete the vital points raised.

(2) It is my belief that the events which took place in the period 1918 to October 1922 and later, required the 'Regime' and successive governments to maintain the pretext that Collins was the greatest Irishman in history by his efforts in the War of Independence, the Treaty and the Civil War. Had they denounced him publicly questions could have been asked concerning the legality of the 'Regime' and any collusion which may have taken place with their British masters and the Catholic bishops. As a result their life, power, wealth and privilege which they had gained by the blood and betrayal of the dead Republicans would have been threatened. The revisionists for the past twenty years have had a total monopoly on the propaganda affecting this most important period in Irish history. I firmly believe that the time is at hand for the truth to surface through the mist of the past and no amount of censorship, black propaganda, misinformation and brainwashing will be sufficient to hold back the tide of the truth which is long overdue.